THE HISTORY OF TEA
BOOK 1

LASZLO MONTGOMERY

The History of Tea Book 1

By Laszlo Montgomery

ISBN-13: 978-988-8843-32-9

© 2023 Laszlo Montgomery

HISTORY / Asia / China

EB197

All rights reserved. No part of this book may be reproduced in material form, by any means, whether graphic, electronic, mechanical or other, including photocopying or information storage, in whole or in part. May not be used to prepare other publications without written permission from the publisher except in the case of brief quotations embodied in critical articles or reviews. For information contact info@earnshawbooks.com

Published in Hong Kong by Earnshaw Books Ltd.

CONTENTS

Introduction	VII
The Tea History Podcast Part 1	1

Welcome to the inaugural episode of Tea History Podcast. Here, we'll be exploring tea's humble beginnings in the Ba and Shu States of ancient Sichuan. We'll also look at the mythical stories surrounding the discovery of tea by the Divine Farmer, Shen Nong.

The Tea History Podcast Part 2	17

Tea's progress as an enjoyable beverage starts to make some headway since Shen Nong's time. But it's still one bitter brew during the Bronze Age centuries. Tea remains a work in progress but showing tremendous promise.

The Tea History Podcast Part 3	31

After centuries of trial and error, the taste of tea starts to transform from a bitter medicinal brew into something worthy of presenting to the emperor as tribute. Tea's rise during the Sui and Tang are introduced this time. The legends behind the critical role tea played in Tibet and other border regions are also discussed.

The Tea History Podcast Part 4	47

In this episode, we finally introduce the Tea Saint. What Elvis was to rock n' roll, Lu Yu was to the popularity of tea in Chinese society. Here we'll look at his life and his celebrated work, "The Classic of Tea". From here on out, tea is no longer tú, and neither is it bitter.

The Tea History Podcast Part 5	59

We looked at Lu Yu in the last episode. This time, we give a once-over to his masterpiece, The Cha Jing or Classic of Tea. The national popularity of tea in China really catches fire after Lu Yu shows everyone how to enjoy it, and enjoy life at the same time.

The Tea History Podcast Part 6   75

In the post-Lu Yu world, tea starts to take off like a rocket. It will take a little longer for tea to get the needed traction in Japan but during the Tang, they get to see it and appreciate it up close. We'll also look at one of the early "Tea Persons", the poet and recluse Lu Tong, as well as one of his most famous tea poems. In this episode, we also introduce the first popular tea ware, Yue ware and Xing ware.

The Tea History Podcast Part 7   91

No longer is tea a bitter brew sharing a Chinese character with the one used for a bitter vegetable. Royals, officials, scholars, and common people are enjoying tea and writing poems inspired by this beverage that has taken China by storm. We also look at one of the greatest royal patrons of tea in Chinese history, the Song Emperor Huizong.

The Tea History Podcast Part 8   107

Buddhism continues to embrace tea even further during the Song Dynasty giving rise to the term 茶禪一味 "Tea and Chan Buddhism are one taste." More Huizong, white tea, Japan's Myōan Eisai, and then we'll close with an introduction to Wulong (Oolong) Tea and the emergence of the Wuyi Mountains in Fujian province as a tea powerhouse.

The Tea History Podcast Part 9   123

The epic story continues after all the great advances in tea production and tea culture in the Song. After surviving the Mongol Yuan Dynasty Camellia Sinensis experiences revolutionary improvements with the founding of the Ming Dynasty by Zhu Yuanzhang. Now tea starts to become more familiar to us after the Hongwu Emperor demands all future tribute teas must be sent in loose-leaf form. With loose leaf teas came greater demands for tea-ware. The history of the kilns of Jingdezhen is introduced, along with their calling card: Blue and White porcelain, China's first global brand. Other innovations such as teas scented with flowers and the Tea Manual of Zhu Quan are also introduced.

The Tea History Podcast Part 10   139

More Ming Dynasty tea history this time. Further innovations from China's tea artisans further improves the taste and experience of tea. The famous "zisha" clay teapots and teaware from Yixing are introduced as well as their role in the Gongfu Tea Ceremony. As the second half of the Ming Dynasty starts to wind down, the Europeans will soon be knocking on China's door. They too will discover the goodness and greatness of tea with historic consequences.

INTRODUCTION

The China History Podcast was launched in June of 2010. The original intention of the show was to offer American people a basic understanding of Chinese history. Recognizing a widespread lack of even the simplest awareness of Chinese history in the USA, Laszlo Montgomery used the relatively new medium of podcasting to make it convenient and easy for listeners to access the show snd satisfy their curiosity to learn about China.

Now more than twelve years later, The China History Podcast is listened to in more than a hundred countries with less than half of the listeners residing in the US. There are over two hundred hours of free content that introduces Chinese history from mythical to modern times. Besides popular Chinese imperial history and post Qing Dynasty history, the China History Podcast has presented hours of content focusing on the lives of Overseas Chinese and their rich history.

The show is listened to all over the world by English-speakers hungry for an entertaining and informative explanation of China's history delivered in an enjoyable non-academic style. So many listeners around the world are Chinese, many of them happy for an entertaining way to reconnect with their heritage.

For more than a decade there have been so many calls from listeners to provide the transcripts to the programs. They will do much to help listeners learn more about China. Laszlo is happy to work with Earnshaw Books to bring you the transcripts from selected shows of The China History Podcast. These will become a unique and enjoyable way to advance English understanding, perhaps re-learn some forgotten history and gain a foreigner's perspective of China's great history presented by someone who has appreciated Chinese culture since he was a small boy growing up in Chicago.

Laszlo Montgomery

 **The Tea History Podcast Book 1 Part 1**

THE TRANSCRIPTS

SUMMARY

Welcome to the inaugural episode of Tea History Podcast. Here, we'll be exploring tea's humble beginnings in the Ba and Shu States of ancient Sichuan. We'll also look at the mythical stories surrounding the discovery of tea by the Divine Farmer, Shen Nong.

TRANSCRIPT

00:00 | Hey everyone, Laszlo Montgomery here. Thanks for joining me in this first episode of the Tea History Podcast.

00:07 | In looking back on the last six years since I presented that tea history series and thinking about all the places tea has taken me, the people I have met along the way and who have taught me so much, I can really understand why tea is called, among other things, a social beverage.

00:25 | Humankind was gifted with three great natural beverages: cocoa, coffee ands tea. And if you don't include the air we breathe and the water we drink, nothing on earth is consumed in greater quantities than tea.

00:39 | Tea wasn't the first of these so-called three great temperance beverages to arrive in Europe. Cocoa came

I

 THE TEA HISTORY PODCAST BOOK 1
PART 1

in 1528…brought there by the great world superpower of the day, España. The Spanish brought it from the New World after the Aztec conquest in 1521.

00:57 | Next up was tea in 1610. Thanks to all Nederlanders for that. Then five years later in 1615 Venetian traders were credited with bringing coffee to Europe from Constantinople.

01:10 | Tea became the first global commodity shipped to markets on six continents. Its history, undeniably, began in Asia. The Golden Triangle region associated in the 20th century with narcotic drugs, was also where the original tea garden was. Tea trees have been around for more than fifty million years.

01:32 | One of the early experts, very much admired in his day and revered by many, on all things tea that is, was William Ukers, whose magnum opus "All about Tea", published in 1935 said, "The original jungles where tea trees grew wild were found in the Shan States of Thailand and East Burma, Yunnan, Northern Vietnam and India. Before all got divided up into nations it was all one big primeval tea garden. Soil, climate, rainfall – everything was perfect to propagate the species."

02:11 | Wherever it was, Yunnan, Sichuan or wherever, the one indisputable historical truth that has made it down to our day is that it was China who acted as the yuántóu, the fountainhead, from whence tea as we know it, came into this world.

THE TEA HISTORY PODCAST BOOK 1
PART 1

02:29 | We'll look at this in more detail much later on but one thing that's not common knowledge but pretty amazing is that no matter where in the world tea is grown or how it is processed, into the darkest, maltiest Assam black tea mixed with milk and sugar or the most subtle tasting white tea using the freshest buds picked before the spring rains in early April selling for a thousand Euros per hundred grams... all tea comes from the same plant. *Camellia sinensis.*

03:01 | *Camellia sinensis* is either a tall tree, a small tree of three to five meters or most often as we've seen before in all those gorgeous photos of tea plantations, a dome-shaped bush of one and a half to three meters high. If you just leave them alone and let them grow wild, a tea tree can grow as high as thirty feet. In the original tea gardens stretching from Sichuan, Yunnan and into the region where Thailand, Laos and Myanmar all come together, there are tea trees hundreds and even thousands of years old spread out over two hundred or so forest areas.

03:42 | The problem with tea trees is that you had to climb them to get to the branches where all the tea leaves were. In time most were all cut down and replaced instead with tea bushes that were much more efficient and much less laborious to cultivate. Then according to the long centuries of accumulated lessons learned through trial and error the tea story unfolds.

04:08 | You'll see, from the earliest times, practically all the way into the Tang Dynasty, 7th to 9th centuries more or less, the kind of tea that was drunk by the ancients probably

 THE TEA HISTORY PODCAST BOOK 1
PART 1

wouldn't be as popular as it is in our day. A good couple thousand years of time passed before the most ancient evenings of China in the Shang and Zhou Bronze Age dynasties to the time in the 7th century when the Tang Dynasty was established in 618 that tea started to taste good.

04:38 Let me read some of the fine print that goes with that sweeping and fantastical botanical claim about all tea leaves being the same. All tea comes from one single species, true, but you have multiple varieties depending on what part of the original tea garden the plant came from. Though the number of cultivars and varietals abound, basically, if you told me to narrow it down to just three, you have the tea leaves that come from the China bush, the Assam bush and the Java bush. And the Java Bush, known as *Camellia sinensis* Cambodi was a transplant of the Assam bush to Java in Indonesia. So really…there's the China and Assam bushes, both a variety of *Camellia sinensis*.

05:23 The leaves of the China bush are smaller than the Assam bush and the China bush can live much longer and can thrive in colder weather. The Assam bush has larger and softer leaves and is a little less hearty than the Chinese varietal and grows best in sub-tropical regions where there's lots of rain. They're the same but not the same.

05:45 The word varietal is usually associated with wine grapes but it's also used in the botanical world as well. The word cultivar is used more often in the tea world. The word was coined by the American horticulturalist

THE TEA HISTORY PODCAST BOOK 1
PART 1

and botanist Liberty Hyde Bailey. Cultivar comes from a combination of the terms cultivated variety. That is to say it isn't a wild plant. It was cultivated.

06:12 This is something that was applied to the *Camellia sinensis* plant throughout Chinese history and is the main reason why you'll hear about there being thousands of different cultivars of the tea plant. In doing this, it allows tea bushes to thrive in very particular areas.

06:32 Back in 1753 Sweden's great botanist Carl Linnaeus published Species Plantarum, the groundbreaking work that gave us the whole scientific nomenclature we still use today. Plant hunters were the Indiana Jones's of their day. They would traverse the world, bring samples back and Linnaeus and those who followed him would classify everything.

06:58 Before it was *Camellia sinensis*, the tea plant was initially classified by Linnaeus as Thea sinensis. In fact, he classified it further as Thea veridis for green tea and Thea bohea for black. No one in Linnaeus's time knew the big secret, that green and black tea came from the same bush.

07:20 The genus for tea was later re-named as part of the Camellia family. There are over 200 species and thousands of cultivars from this Camellia family of evergreens.

THE TEA HISTORY PODCAST BOOK 1
PART 1

07:32 So, tea trees and plants had always been around from pre-recorded history's earliest days but the secrets of the leaf remained undiscovered. It took someone to have that first a-ha moment when, after consuming these particular leaves, they caught that first buzz or moment of pleasure. But it wasn't enough simply to be cognizant of the sensation. Someone also had to pass the word around the forest and let others know about this beverage. And then these others would in turn pass this information on even further, maybe to more distant lands.

08:05 Even the most bitter tea was cause for ripples of excitement to spread through the hills, valleys and forests of Southeast Asia. Back in those Neolithic days there were great discoveries being made every day in the forests, along the rivers, on the plains, in the mountains and wherever humans were congregating. Sometimes word spread of certain discoveries. Sometimes the chance discovery was made but didn't get propagated and humankind would have to wait another thousand years to rediscover it. As we'll see from the earliest mentions about tea, the Chinese had already noticed from the start that these tea leaves, when boiled in water, perked you up a bit.

08:48 Historians for a thousand years and more have combed through documents searching for the earliest references of the *Camellia sinensis* plant. Prior to 2016 all we had to go on was a copy of a document called the Tóngyuē, "A Contract with a Servant." Listed among the various terms of this contract it noted tea utensils and called for

THE TEA HISTORY PODCAST BOOK 1
PART 1

someone to go down to Chengdu, capital of Sichuan, and to secure a servant who would perform an itemized list of services. And among the tasks requested of this servant to perform involved buying, brewing, and serving tea.

09:29 Furthermore this document credited to a certain Wáng Bāo, mentioned the town of Wǔyáng in Sichuan province not far from Chéngdū. This is where China's oldest known central tea market was located.

09:42 So all the way up to very recently a reliable record of tea's existence in China only went back as far as 59 BCE....2,080 years ago.

09:54 But it was only five years ago in 2016 that Chinese archaeologists combing through the tomb of Emperor Jǐng of Hàn, Hàn Jǐngdì, they found the earliest traces of tea leaves. Emperor Jǐng reigned from 157 to 141 BCE which means this tea they found was more than two thousand one hundred years old and predated the mention of tea in that Tóngyuē contract. Here were actual tea leaves, well aged indeed.

10:28 So, although we're pretty sure tea was around even longer than twenty-one hundred years ago, we now have archaeological evidence that proves it was at least as far back as the fourth Hàn Emperor Jǐng, father of the great Hàn Wǔdì, that we can accurately point to tea's existence in China.

THE TEA HISTORY PODCAST BOOK 1
PART 1

10:45 | Before tea became known as chá in Mandarin it went through several name changes. Before there was chá, there were five other names for tea: Jiǎ, Tú, Chuǎn, Shè and Míng.

11:00 | The patron saint, whose life and work we will look at in later episodes was Lù Yǔ. He lived during the heyday of the Táng Dynasty. His great work was the Chá Jīng, or Classic of Tea. For now, I just want to briefly mention him. Lù Yǔ was sort of, if I may, the Elvis of wénrén or literary people who wrote about tea. From the time of Lù Yǔ and the Chá Jīng, all the way into our present day there have been many other great tea treatises, guides and studies that followed. But Chinese have always put Lù Yǔ in a class by himself. He was the King. The Chá Shèng, the Tea Saint. Again, for such a figure as Lù Yǔ and the great impact he had on tea, I've dedicated a whole episode to him. So stay tuned for that when we get to the Táng Dynasty.

11:53 | But tea goes way back much further than Lù Yǔ and the Táng Dynasty. How far back you might be wondering. Well, it was way before Chinese recorded history began. This involves the legend of Shén Nóng. Lù Yǔ said Shén Nóng, the Divine Farmer, among other names, he was the one who discovered tea.

12:12 | If you believe the myth, it all started in the 2700's BCE. In less than 200 years there would be an army of workers and artisans commencing their work on the Great Pyramid in Giza. This was also the age of cuneiform writing in the Fertile Crescent, modern day Iraq and Syria. This was

THE TEA HISTORY PODCAST BOOK 1
PART 1

also the time when Stonehenge was built.

12:35 Well over in China, presumably somewhere along the Yellow River there was Shén Nóng, the second of the Three Sovereigns I mentioned. In China folk culture, he's about as big as you can get. He's graced the covers of a lot of calendars over the millennia. Shén Nóng, Fúxī, the Yellow Emperor. That's the Holy Trinity of China's most ancient mythical rulers, or sovereigns.

13:00 Chinese folk tradition mentioned from the earliest times that it was Shén Nóng who first noticed that tea leaves brewed in hot water gave you a buzz. The Incas of the 6th century figured out the same thing from chewing coca leaves. And so it may have been with tea leaves in China. It was probably someone chewing on the leaves who noticed that first mini jolt rather than the Shén Nóng version of the story.

13:27 But let's tell it anyway.

13:29 What is there to say about Shén Nóng? He brought agriculture to China. He's the father of Chinese Medicine and left behind a magnificent work called the Shén Nóng Běncǎo Jīng, The Divine Farmer's Materia Medica or simply the Shen Nong Herbal. This great work, who knows who compiled it, it probably came out around the time of the Three Kingdoms period…3rd century CE. It was a collection of what everyone knew up to that point about plants, agriculture and medicine. Shen Nong is also credited with inventing the Chinese calendar. I mean, he's big.

 THE TEA HISTORY PODCAST BOOK 1
PART 1

14:07 | Shén Nóng also brought us the secrets of tea to mankind. How did he do such a thing? There are multiple versions, the most famous of which I will tell. The reason Shén Nóng was able to write himself into the history books was mainly due to his willingness to stick his neck out and try out different plants and herbs to test their effects on his body.

14:31 | As anyone who saw the 2007 movie directed by Sean Penn called "Into the Wild", doing this kind of thing is risky and life threatening to say the least. But through trial and error and some good fortune, Shén Nóng compiled quite a long list of herbal remedies that did wonders for a multitude of ailments and afflictions of the day.

14:52 | There's this story of Shén Nóng tasting a hundred plants. This came straight from Lù Yǔ. Shén Nóng was out walking one day and decided to sit down and rest, so tired and thirsty was he from all his work. He boiled some water in his pot. This was what people did back then. The Chinese figured that one out real early. Boil the water first; get sick and die less often.

15:18 | So Shen Nong was boiling his water when lo and behold several leaves from the tea tree he was sitting under blew into his cup. Of course, as far back as Shén Nóng's day it was a tea tree and not a bush. Since no one had discovered tea yet, the trees were all lush and wild and growing everywhere in China's southwest where Shén Nóng was wandering at the time. Shen Nong no doubt took these leaves falling into his pot as a good sign and

THE TEA HISTORY PODCAST BOOK 1
PART 1

tasted that natural brew. It quenched his thirst, gave him a nice pick-me-up and left him feeling all refreshed.

15:53 Another story about Shén Nóng goes, and this is a variation of the Shén Nóng tasting a hundred plants and herbs tale, that when Shén Nóng tried those hundred plants, seventy-two of them turned out to be toxic. And as he lay on the ground after ingesting some poisonous shrub or fruit, possibly dying and knock knock knocking on heaven's door, you know what happened next. Some tea leaves from a nearby tea tree blew off the branches and landed right within reach of The Divine Farmer. He consumed these leaves and suddenly he was feeling in tip-top shape.

16:30 Shén Nóng grabbed a basket and plucked and gathered as many of these leaves as he could carry. He consumed more of them and slowly all the poisons from the six dozen kinds of toxic flora he tested were all purged from his body. So Shén Nóng did a lot of research into this and passed this good word on to all the people in the land.

16:52 And as far as Lù Yǔ is concerned, we all have Shén Nóng to thank for enlightening the world about the health benefits derived from tea.

17:00 There's another story that says Shén Nóng discovered tea when he came upon a burning tea bush and noticed the fragrance of the burning and roasting leaves. It grabbed his attention and in no time at all he learned how to get this type of bush to yield its magical elixir.

THE TEA HISTORY PODCAST BOOK 1
PART 1

17:17 Shen Nong being a folk god extraordinaire so to speak, has about a million other legends and stories associated with him depending on which village you come from in China. With this defining historical legend concerning Shén Nóng and the discovery of tea, China has pretty much claimed squatters' rights with respect to who brought tea to the world.

17:40 The thing about tea in Shén Nóng's time and pretty much all the way up to the Zhōu Dynasty, was that it was more of a medicine than something you might make for yourself just to kick back and chill. Zhou Dynasty tea was supposedly very bitter, very heavy, even viscous. Tea as we know it, in the time of the Zhōu kings, still had a long way to go.

18:05 Shén Nóng wrote of tea in his Běncǎo Jīng: "Tea tastes bitter. Drinking it, one can think quicker, sleep less, move more nimbly, and see more clearly." Coming from someone the likes of Shén Nóng, that's quite an endorsement. And Shén Nóng, who would have carried a Chinese passport, by extension, passed on no small amount of glory to the motherland for being the one to discover such a miracle and wonder.

18:33 I read Shén Nóng left his earthly form in Húnán province at a place called Tea Hill, or Chálín. There must be some element of truth to this because I found the Chálín on Google Maps. It's a little bit northeast of Zhāngjiājiè. So you know The Divine Farmer passed away in some beautiful surroundings. No mention if he went by natural causes or was poisoned to death.

THE TEA HISTORY PODCAST BOOK 1
PART 1

18:58 Shén Nóng didn't call tea chá yet. Way back then tea was called tú 荼. Shén Nóng wasn't kidding when he said it was bitter. People familiar with Chinese characters will note that tú, second tone, is written exactly like the character chá but with one extra horizontal stroke. You can hardly notice it if you don't look closely. Like rù 入 and rén 人, The character tú looks very similar to chá and it was natural that the character for tea, chá ultimately be derived from the character tú.

19:34 Users of the Liáng Shíqiū Chinese-English Dictionary, my stalwart going back to the 1980's, will note tú is character 4931. It stands for the *Sonchus oleraceus*, a vegetable also called in Chinese kǔcài. It's also known as sow-thistle or smart-wood. At least during the Later Han, 23 to 220 CE this vegetable called tú had a dual usage, meaning tea as well.

20:04 In ancient writings where the character tú comes up, like the Book of Songs and Book of Rites, the Shījīng and Lǐjì, historians had to be sure what kind of tú it was they were reading in the texts? The bitter tasting vegetable or the ancient name of tea, which was also bitter. You know, there's always smoke everywhere you go in ancient China. Historians want to behold the fire, not the smoke. The hard part was simply to find documents that had the character tú. Then scholars would expend all their energies to figure out from the context, are they talking about chá, tea or kǔcài bitter vegetable?

20:42 Around the year 725 when chá forever more replaced tú as the word for tea, no one told the folks in Fújiàn

THE TEA HISTORY PODCAST BOOK 1
PART 1

province and they kept on calling it tú or in that part of China, tay. And in their various Mǐn dialects tú came out sounding like tea. So, when the first Western traders came to China, off the coast of Fújiàn, they asked what's this stuff called? And their Hokkien and Hokchiu suppliers told them in their own dialects, it's called tay. And as far as the first Europeans were concerned, tay it became.

21:16 Now down in Guǎngdōng province, southernmost China, including the capital Guǎngzhōu or Canton, they had heard about the name change when it happened and therefore tea was chá down there. So everyone who ended up buying tea out of Canton knew it as chá or some variation thereof. And all those, like the Dutch and Portuguese who did their purchasing out of Xiàmén, Fúzhōu, Quánzhōu or wherever along the coast of Fújiàn, they knew it as tea.

21:46 And since we in the West have the Dutch to thank for being the first Europeans to engage in the tea biz and bring it to the continent, we know it as tea rather than chá. They were the first-to-market and as it often went in history, they got naming rights.

22:02 I mentioned that in 59 BCE during the time of the Western Han emperor Xuān there was a mention of tea in this Wáng Bāo document that was discovered. At the outset of the 2nd century there was another work discovered called the Shuōwén Jiězì. It came out during the reign of Eastern Hàn Emperor Āndì.

THE TEA HISTORY PODCAST BOOK 1
PART 1

22:23 This Shuōwén Jiězì, this was a Chinese dictionary to end all dictionaries that analyzed all the known Chinese characters to date. Tea was referred to as míng and was described as buds picked from the tú plant. There are no surviving copies of the Shuōwén Jiězì. When are there ever? So many of these millennia old documents perished throughout the ages. Like it is for a lot of these Chinese ancient works, we know of the Shuōwén Jiězì and about its contents from the documents and compendia that followed later on and referred to it and quoted it.

23:00 But from looking at this document from 121 AD, the time of Hadrian in Rome, we can at least deduce that the Chinese had figured out the buds were the best part of the tea plant and that if you plucked them, more shoots would sprout forth. Today some of the most prized and pricey green and white teas only contain the buds. Seems they also felt the same way two thousand years ago.

23:26 Rather than start yakking about the next thing on my mind, let's pull down the curtain and call it a night until next time.

23:32 Thanks for listening everyone. Laszlo Montgomery here signing off from Los Angeles California, same city where the China History Podcast is produced in fact. We share the same recording studio. You might want to check that out one out. It's considered one of the best China History flavored podcasts out there.

THE TEA HISTORY PODCAST BOOK 1
PART 1

23:51 | Well, we managed to get this first episode out of the way. I cordially invite you to consider coming back next time for what I'm predicting will be another tasty episode of the Tea History Podcast.

The Tea History Podcast Book 1 Part 2

SUMMARY

Tea's progress as an enjoyable beverage starts to make some headway since Shen Nong's time. But it's still one bitter brew during the Bronze Age centuries. Tea remains a work in progress but showing tremendous promise.

TRANSCRIPT

00:00 Welcome back my friends to the show that never ends. Laszlo Montgomery here with the second episode of this kind of but not entirely brand new podcast, as if the history podcasting space wasn't crowded enough already.

00:12 Don't forget to check out the China History Podcast if you haven't already. It's definitely one of the best Chinese history-related podcasts shows out there….or so I've been told.

00:25 Let's pick up where we left off last time, the Zhōu Dynasty. When you talk about ancient China, man, this is as ancient as it comes. There was maybe the Xià Dynasty and for sure there was the Shāng. But Chinese civilization, Chinese culture as we recognize it in our day, this is where it all started, Zhōu Dynasty. Lǎozǐ, Confucius, Kings Wén and Wǔ, the Duke of Zhōu, Hán

 THE TEA HISTORY PODCAST BOOK 1
PART 2

Fēizǐ, Mèngzǐ, Guǎn Zhòng and Duke Huán of Qí. The first emperor Qín Shǐhuáng, he was born during the last decades of the Eastern Zhōu, during the Warring States Period.

01:05　The Shang Dynasty is famous for the Oracle Bones and the artifacts dug out of the Ruins of Yīn, the Yīn Xū outside Ānyáng in Hénán Province, right on the Yellow River, where it all began for the Chinese Huáxià civilization.

01:25　The Zhōu dynasty saw the introduction of the three great religions of China: Confucianism, Daoism and Buddhism. All three showed up on the scene roughly during the same time during the Eastern Zhōu. And all three religions will embrace tea not so much for the taste as much as for the health benefits, the rituals they will associate with its preparation and consumption and the ability to offer a nice pick-me-up when needed. One religious sect in particular, Chán Buddhism, known in Japan as Zen Buddhism incorporated tea into the religion itself.

02:05　I include Buddhism in this group of Chinese religions even though it came from India. This religion early on, as it wended its way around China, discovered the merits of tea and how it served as a perfect antidote for thirst, fatigue and a myriad of life's ills and pleasures. And we'll see in the episodes to come how some of the greatest teas that Chinese masters will ever produce got their start in these Buddhist temples.

THE TEA HISTORY PODCAST BOOK 1
PART 2

02:38 Tea's journey from a novel discovery to a medicinal plant took its sweet time. Historians and archaeologists have uncovered all kinds of mentions of tea. There is a mention of tea being sent from Yunnan in 1066 BCE as a gift to the King. This would have been the infamous and final King of the Shāng Dynasty, Zhòu Xīn. Yes, the wine pool and meat forest king, among other torture devices.

03:09 Yúnnán has the oldest tea trees around. I read 1,700 years old. They've been using tea in Yúnnán at least since the Shāng Dynasty and had been boiling the leaves along with a variety of other natural products of the forest.

03:26 I spent an afternoon once drinking tea in Chéngdū with a lovely couple at their tea shop. Boy, they sure knew a lot about tea. He was from Fúzhōu and his wife was local to Chéngdū. Anyways he showed me a photo he took in front of a tree in a secret location in Yúnnán that he said was almost 3,000 years old.

03:46 As far as China's recorded history goes, in the Shāng Dynasty, tea was certainly around and was being offered as tribute to the Chinese king from Yúnnán where tea production was said to have first started. Tea was something that would spread south to north. At this nascent stage of tea's history there was no Chinese character for tea invented yet up in the north where Shang civilization was. So there's nothing written about tea in the oracle bones or the earliest bronze ware. Knowledge of tea was still a secret south of the Yángzǐ River.

THE TEA HISTORY PODCAST BOOK 1
PART 2

04:23 | There's also the Gān Lù legend. This is the story of Wú Lǐzhēn. He lived during the time of the Western Han and Emperor Xuān 汉宣帝. The legend has it that Wú Lǐzhēn was on his way back from India after a stint studying Buddhism down there, around 53 BCE. This was a common thing to do back then, these pilgrimages to the source of Buddhist teachings.

04:48 | Somewhere along the way, Wú Lǐzhēn had taken cuttings from seven tea trees and was carefully transporting them back to his home in Sichuan. And when he got to a certain spot on Méngdǐng Mountain, Méngdǐng Shān in Sichuan, he planted these seven tea plants. This is about 125 km southwest of Chengdu.

05:15 | Then after some time had passed and once these small trees were mature and ready, Wú Lǐzhēn regularly took cuttings from these original seven trees and over time these cuttings were planted all over Méngdǐng Mountain and he created a kind of tea heaven.

05:33 | And this particular tea snipped from these trees growing in the primordial tea forest somewhere around Yunnan today, that Wú Lǐzhēn had hand-carried all the way and planted on Méngdǐng Shan, from the original seven trees, came this yellow colored Méngdǐng Gān Lù cha. Gān Lù Tea. And so pleasant was this brew, in no time at all it became too special for the common people and was henceforth reserved solely for the emperor.

06:05 | Gān Lù Tea also became known as Xiān Chá, the tea of the immortals. Because of Wú Lǐzhēn and his seven trees,

THE TEA HISTORY PODCAST BOOK 1
PART 2

this area in Sichuan southwest of Chengdu, in Yǎ'ān and Qiónglái, a nice ninety minute to two-hour car ride, is called the birthplace of tea cultivation in China. This is where it most likely all began.

06:30 The original seven tea bushes planted by Wú Lǐzhēn are no doubt long gone. But you can still visit the spot where tradition said these original seven trees stand today, protected of course. We know that gingko trees were also planted in the same exact spot at the same time, and that these trees have been reliably dated to more than two thousand years ago.

06:55 Since at least the time of the Zhōu dynasty, tea was already well-known to Buddhist monks. Performing all those daily devotions, sometimes these monks, even the abbot, they needed something to give them a natural boost to help them carry on throughout the day and do good deeds and keep on keeping on.

07:15 Tea became the answer early on. Buddhist temples were all aware of tea and cherished the tea plant not just as a beverage and for its rejuvenating benefits, but also as a health product that, when mixed together with various other herbs and natural substances, provided medicinal relief or prevention of all kinds of Zhōu and Hàn Dynasty ailments.

07:40 Tea in these first centuries of the Common Era still hadn't become a fanciful and enjoyable beverage yet. Not even for the aristocracy. They learned a few tricks in the Han Dynasty. They learned that steaming the tea leaves and

THE TEA HISTORY PODCAST BOOK 1
PART 2

then drying them before compressing the leaves into bricks helped cut down the bitterness. This was a big advancement. The spoilage was astronomical. Prior to steaming the leaves, they used to dry them by exposing them to charcoal fires. With these meager advances, tea remained bitter and was mostly consumed as part of some brew containing other natural ingredients.

08:21 In the Records of the Three Kingdoms, the Sānguó Zhì, considered the definitive source material for all things Three Kingdoms period, there's also a clear mention about tea that assures us in our day, again, that the Chinese in the 3rd century knew of tea.

08:40 There's also a rather well-known story about the drunken Wú King, Sūn Hào, grandson of Sūn Quán. This is an ancient tea tale. King Sūn Hào had a loyal scholar, historian and courtier named Wéi Yào. His bio states in the Sānguó Zhì, the Record of the Three Kingdoms, that because Wéi Yào had a weak constitution and in no way could hold his own in King Sūn Hào's frequent bacchanals, he was allowed to yǐ chá dài jiǔ, to drink tea instead of wine. The good king cut him some slack...

09:17 Even today at some of these events where people gather and drink themselves into oblivion, if there's someone who clearly will not be able to participate, the host will let them off the hook and allow them to yǐ chá dài jiǔ, to substitute tea for alcohol. When I used to frequent these business dinners and banquets with all these officials, there was always someone doing yǐ chá dài jiǔ.

THE TEA HISTORY PODCAST BOOK 1
PART 2

09:41 | Like I said, all we have to go on in these earliest days are snippets here and there of these minor but definitive references to tea.

09:50 | You probably recall from previous episodes that when the Jìn Dynasty fell and northern China was taken over by Mongol and Turkic tribes, a lot of the northern elites and aristocrats of the day, seeing dark times ahead, picked up and moved south. This was the first time in Chinese history a human migration from north to south happened on such a mass scale as this.

10:15 | Tea was already a familiar thing down in the south where it grew naturally. Now these northern aristocrats fleeing to the south after the fall of the Jìn, got to see up close for the first time what this was all about. This is how tea grew.

10:31 | Even though tea, or tú as it was still called, had been around for so long, no one in China had yet figured out how to unlock all the magic contained inside the cells of the tea leaves. Tea's rise during the periods of the Shāng-Zhōu-Hàn and through to the Jìn continued to grow in esteem amongst the Chinese as a stimulant and something natural that had acquired a reputation for ameliorating all kinds of ills. And like I said, during the Eastern Zhou when all the three religions of China embraced tea, that too had a great impact on awareness about tea.

11:12 | Tea came from the southwest of China. That much was clear. Yunnan and Sìchuān. That was about as far away

THE TEA HISTORY PODCAST BOOK 1
PART 2

as you could get from Luòyáng or Cháng'ān. So those places never really fell under the tight control of the central government. The Qin State and later the dynasty were the first ones to go down there and crack a whip and get everybody on board. And it's not surprising that the Qín conquests of the southwest opened the door to the introduction of tea in greater quantities, as a tribute commodity, into the north of China.

11:47 | The oldest surviving Chinese encyclopedia dates back to 350, the peak of the Eastern Jìn Dynasty. Right after the death of Constantine the Great in the West. It's known as the Ěr Yǎ. This work is a pretty sacred text because it's attributed, at least in part, to the Duke of Zhou and Confucius. It explained, in all the detail and authority possible at the time, about words, family relations, utensils, heaven, earth, the hills and mountains, plants, trees, animals of all kinds and animal husbandry. In the Ěr Yǎ, tea is also specifically mentioned.

12:30 | It described tea as Jiǎ 檟, third tone, that was the word for tea. Jiǎ. It was described in the Ěr Yǎ this way, "The plant is a small tree, like a gardenia. The leaves grown in the winter may be boiled to make a soup for drinking. Nowadays, those that are gathered late are called míng 茗. Another name for them is chuǎn 荈. The people of Shǔ (meaning present day Sichuan) call them kǔ tú 苦荼".

12:59 | Kǔ Tú could be translated as bitter tea.

24

THE TEA HISTORY PODCAST BOOK 1
PART 2

13:20 All these ancient names for tea are said to have begun with the good people of Sìchuān. If you visit the wonderful National Tea Museum in Hangzhou not far from the tea gardens of Lóngjǐng, you'll see, they say it was the Bā-Shǔ people of present-day Sichuan province and the municipality of Chóngqìng who get credit for being the first ones to basically figure out tea. By the time of the Ěr Yǎ it was known people in southwest China were cultivating tea.

13:32 Before the Kingdom of Qin, led by Qín Shǐhuáng, united all of China, they first had to knock off all their opponents. In 316 BCE, fifty-six years before the birth of Yíng Zhèng, the Qín sent their military machine down to the southwest. And they rolled in to the Kingdoms of the Bā and Shǔ and folded that area into the unified China that they were cobbling together, conquest by conquest. And along with all the other agricultural riches of this one day Sìchuān province were all its tea trees and cultivation know-how.

14:11 And thanks to the Qin conquest in the 4th century BCE and later on after Yíng Zhèng beat off his last rival and unified the land, he declared himself China's first emperor. And as far as all that culture and all the other good things from Sichuan, including tea, all of that began to more naturally flow northward, albeit slowly, towards the central plain, to all the major cities and towns of the Yellow River and its many tributaries, already ancient by this time.

THE TEA HISTORY PODCAST BOOK 1
PART 2

14:43 | Again, this wasn't the tea you and I would be familiar with, but that would change of course.

14:49 | And this is how tea first became well known in central and north China. What started off as a Sichuan and Yunnan thing, down in the southwest of China, deep in the interior, thanks to thousands of years of horticultural advancement, was now and over the next several centuries, being planted, studied and wholly embraced by those Chinese people who got to enjoy it for the first time.

15:17 | And although it was Yunnan and Sichuan who gave China tea, it would later on end up being the tea gardens in eastern China, Anhui, Fujian, Zhejiang, Jiangxi and Jiangsu who planted the seeds and cuttings from ground zero in Sichuan and Yunnan and developed their own teas, that would later become world renowned and their leaves would be sought after by connoisseurs the world over, commanding prices in the thousands of dollars per kilo.

15:49 | Yeah, but in the time of the Zhou, the Qin and into the Han, tea was still a bitter brew, man. And though it gave the imbiber a nice little buzz and perhaps some solace and enjoyment, bitterness was still its defining characteristic. In this 3rd and 4th century BCE world, tea, or tú, or chuǎn, or shè or míng, it sure was bitter and mostly a health product and a luxury only afforded by the rich.

THE TEA HISTORY PODCAST BOOK 1
PART 2

16:20 No one had figured out quite yet how to process the leaves into an enjoyable beverage. The drink that Zhou, Qin and Han era people were ingesting came from leaves straight from the tree and then later added into your cup of boiled water, Shen Nong style.

16:38 Following the Er Ya of the Zhou was another great work called the Guǎngyǎ that came out in the 3rd century CE during the Three Kingdoms period. This was another work filled with commentaries and updates to previous renditions of the Er Ya. The Guǎngyǎ was a good example of a compendium that was produced to bring previous scholarship up to date. Scholars will keep doing this throughout the centuries in China. Every century or so, some great work would be commissioned by the emperor to bring the extent of human knowledge up to date, and later on for literature as well.

17:16 Here in the Guǎngyǎ, for the first time, we can read the following: "In the district between the province of Hubei and Sichuan the leaves are plucked and made into cakes. Those made of old leaves are mixed with rice. To make tea as a drink, bake the cake until reddish in color, pound it into tiny pieces, put in a chinaware pot. Pour boiling water over them and add onion, ginger, and orange. The drink renders one sober from intoxication and keeps one awake." Sounds more like a soup than a beverage, but everything was moving in the right direction.

17:56 As I mentioned during the Qin, tea started to make its way northward and eastward. And later on with the victories of Han Wudi and China's whole integration

THE TEA HISTORY PODCAST BOOK 1
PART 2

with worlds beyond their borders via the Silk Roads, this facilitated the introduction of tea to others whose world came in contact with China. That, too, caused the repute of tea to travel even farther and wider. As I said, tea masters during the Han had brought their craft to a more refined state than their predecessors, but it wasn't yet a nice tasty brew to look forward to in the morning or afternoon.

18:35 The Liu Song Dynasty (420-479) is about as early as we can reliably trace where the idea of real tribute tea began. This whole notion of tribute tea is important. What this involved was sending the best tea in the land to the emperor as a gift, for his private use. Even though he was the emperor, he was still a man and a man can only drink so much. So he had way more than he needed. And one of the perks of working for the emperor was you also had access to these teas that were given as tribute. And not only the court official got to drink it, but his family and sometimes his friends as well.

19:16 You remember the Liu Song Dynasty. They're not the Northern or Southern Song who came later. The Liu Song was the first of the southern dynasties during the Southern and Northern Dynasties Period, 420-589, that preceded the Suí. During the Liu Song it was written, "Twenty li from the city of Wùchéng in Zhejiang there is the Wen Mountain which grows the tea reserved for the emperor as tribute tea."

THE TEA HISTORY PODCAST BOOK 1
PART 2

19:46 So 5th century CE not only has the cultivation of tea spread from Yunnan and Sichuan to the east of China, it is also becoming something so prized and valuable. It became worthy enough to be sent to the emperor as a gift.

20:01 The great teas of China today, the ones you see for sale in dozens of web sites or tea shops, all the most prized tea in all of China pretty much all of them started their brilliant career as an imperial Tribute Tea. And from this reputation, a particular village whose masterwork created the tea, would gain legendary status and repute for being a tribute tea supplier to the emperor. And their tea would be even more prized and valued throughout the land.

20:33 Later on, we'll look at most of these great and legendary tribute teas and I'll let you know how you too can get your hands on a few hundred grams for your own personal consumption, just like His Royal Majesty.

20:44 If you had to do or die and draw a line where tea for sure began to be drunk as a beverage and not only as a medicine, the Sui Dynasty would have to be it. From the time of the Three Kingdoms, into the Jin and later on the disunity that followed in the Nanbei Chao, the Southern and Northern Dynasties, man, I'm telling you a lot can happen in 360 years.

21:08 During these years between the time of Zhuge Liang, Yang Jiān and Sui Wendi, the knowledge and wisdom of tea had advanced to a point where the drink started to become a true art and a muse that will spawn a million poems and paintings. But keep in mind even though tea as a beverage turned a corner around the Sui Dynasty, it was still a brick tea world and would remain so for several more centuries yet.

21:37 Next episode we'll focus on the Tang Dynasty, 618-907. Here is where tea finally comes of age and those parts of the world within China's influence, gets hooked. So that's all for next time.

21:51 Until then, this is Laszlo Montgomery signing off from fantastic LA located here in the Golden State, California USA. Take care everyone, and I hope you'll come back again next time for another flavorful episode of the Tea History Podcast.

The Tea History Podcast
Book 1 Part 3

THE TRANSCRIPTS

SUMMARY

After centuries of trial and error, the taste of tea starts to transform from a bitter medicinal brew into something worthy of presenting to the emperor as tribute. Tea's rise during the Sui and Tang are introduced this time. The legends behind the critical role tea played in Tibet and other border regions are also discussed.

TRANSCRIPT

00:00 | Hey everyone, Laszlo Montgomery here, back again with Part 3. On behalf of everyone here at the Tea History Podcast, welcome back.

00:09 | Last episode we looked back on tea's most ancient origins in Chinese history. No one knows for sure who that first Chárén *or "tea person"* was who lived where the tea trees grew indigenously between the Brahmaputra Valley in the west and Sichuan Province in the east. Who was that tea person who first discovered the delights yielded by these leaves and became its first apostle? Let me quote William Ukers who put it so nicely,

00:39 | *"The Chinese learned the use of the tea drink of the aboriginal tribesmen of the hill districts bordering on Southwestern China. These tribesmen occasionally prepared a beverage by boiling raw, green leaves of wild tea trees in kettles over*

THE TEA HISTORY PODCAST BOOK 1
PART 3

smoky, outdoor fires. This was the earliest, crude beginning of what the Chinese and Japanese later developed into a socio-religious rite of exquisite refinement."

01:08 Until we know better, Shén Nóng, the Divine Farmer mentioned in Part 1 is standing in for that person. But at least from the beginnings of recorded history, the Shang Dynasty, we know at least that tea was already around. It was bitter. It wasn't called chá. Its value was primarily as a medicine. If anyone drank it for pleasure, they sure hadn't popularized it yet.

01:34 It was learned early on that steaming the leaves first before pounding them into cakes of tea not only improved the storage technology but also made the tea a little less bitter. The old method of drying the leaves involved charring them, which left a bitter aftertaste in one's mouth.

01:51 It took a long time to figure out even the crudest ways to work the freshly plucked leaves. But figure it out they did, and as tea began to lose some of its edge one began to see the possibilities of tea as a beverage.

02:06 From several previous China History Podcast episodes, you no doubt recall that so much of the Táng Dynasty was rooted in the achievements of the father-son team of Suí Wéndì and Suí Yángdì. Their Suí Dynasty didn't last too long, 581-618, not even forty years. But they got a lot done, including most famously The Grand Canal. They knew how to spend money, I'll give them that.

THE TEA HISTORY PODCAST BOOK 1
PART 3

02:33 Tea's transition from medicine to beverage began during the Sui. Right about here. The distance from the fall of Suí Emperor Yáng and the birth of Lù Yǔ was only a hundred and fifteen years. So the Suí is considered the transitionary period where tea, as we'd recognize it today, started to happen.

02:55 The common way to drink tea back then was still to add stuff to it. Adding spices, fruits, plum juice or ginger to the tea was one way to cut into the bitterness, or at least distract you from it.

03:09 By the 7th century, the process of making tea had reached a point where not only did it win acceptance from the local people, it was also a massive hit with all the peoples who bordered China, to the southwest in Tibet, to the west into Central Asia, and to the north in Mongolia.

03:28 Now with a healthy demand being ramped up in these border regions, and the Silk Roads already well-worn for at least eight centuries, tea started to become a very big business for some. This naturally put demands on quality, packaging, transport and product differentiation. And to facilitate all this, a transport system also needed to be created.

03:53 Remember CHP-111 on the Wú State, King Fūchāi late fifth century BCE. This king of Wú built the Hán Canal, the Hán Gōu, which connected the Huái and Yángzǐ Rivers. It was quite a feat in its day.

 THE TEA HISTORY PODCAST BOOK 1
PART 3

04:10 | And when Emperor Yáng of Suí expanded Fūchāi's Hán Canal into the Grand Canal, stretching from all the way from Beijing to Hangzhou, this opened up the floodgates for domestic trade and commerce in China. And because the Grand Canal was an Eastern China technological and transportation marvel, the whole center of gravity for the tea trade shifted slowly eastward.

04:35 | The tea forests of southwest China started to become less important. Their role became more about satiating the markets of the border regions like Tibet and Central Asia. Since tea for these people was more of a beverage than something to wax eloquent over with one's highbrow friends, their demands on quality didn't do too much to spur innovation. It would be in the eastern provinces of Fújiàn, Zhèjiāng, Ānhuī and Jiāngxī where things were brought to a high art.

05:08 | After the Jìn Dynasty fell in 420, many of these Northern aristocrats ended up migrating en masse in a southerly direction and began settling down in all the choicest areas of Jiāngsū and Zhèjiāng. And in the case of the Hakka people, they ended up in eastern Guǎngdōng and western Fújiàn.

05:28 | It was only natural that these places would become so prominent and would so wholeheartedly embrace tea. And no offense to northern China but the south of China, south of the Yangzi River, that's where all the gorgeous landscape painting-worthy places were located. It's no wonder that it was during this age that Chinese landscape painting as we know it today, was

THE TEA HISTORY PODCAST BOOK 1
PART 3

born. Jiāngsū, Zhèjiāng, parts of Ānhuī and Fújiàn. Those places were simply too intoxicating to the elites, artists and scholars of the day.

06:05 And as it turned out, there were lots of shaded hilly places in the east of China with excellent soil drainage and the right temperatures and climate. So although they continued to grow and produce tea in Sìchuān, Guìzhōu and Yúnnán to this very day, later on we'll see it will be the teas coming out of the eastern provinces that would shake the world and give pleasures and inspiration to who knows how many tea connoisseurs.

06:33 For the first two thousand years we really had to glean through the historical record to understand some of the most basic things about tea and about how far its development had come. Now in the Tang dynasty so many things will happen so quickly, especially after Táng Tàizōng, the dynasty co-founder, pacified the western borders and brought the Silk Road to even greater heights, never seen before.

07:00 In the Táng Dynasty, tea is going to finally begin to go down-market. Rather than remain a drink for the haves, it will now be easily assessable to the have-nots. And though tea had always been treated and handled like a commodity, now it starts to become much fancier and refined stuff. And this required all kinds of tea ware, tools and utensils designed specifically for tea.

 THE TEA HISTORY PODCAST BOOK 1
PART 3

07:28 Tea become more refined and fancy in the Táng. It had been adopted both by Buddhists and scholars and served as a muse and a medium to further enjoy la dolce vita. In Chinese history Táng poets are particularly revered and remembered for the great heights they brought their craft. Many great poems were dedicated to tea. We'll look at one later.

07:53 If you want to go check out the China History Podcast, you'll find a pretty halfway decent six-part series on the History of Chinese Poetry. I humbly recommend that.

08:04 The reputation of tea became particularly well known in the regions bordering Táng China, Tibet, Qīnghǎi, and Xīnjiāng. These people couldn't live without it. Not only was it a beverage that was essential to their daily happiness and enjoyment, it was even more essential for the health benefits it conveyed to people who lived in places so inhospitable, growing enough vegetables to sustain a community was out of the question.

08:34 The demand beyond China's borders was quite great. To facilitate the transport of tea to the roof of the world and up to the northwest of China into Xinjiang and Mongolia, routes were created where caravans of men and horses traversed west and north, bringing mostly Chinese tea to the daily lives of the Himalayan people. These routes became known as the Chámǎ Gǔdào, the Ancient Tea-Horse Road.

THE TEA HISTORY PODCAST BOOK 1
PART 3

09:04 And during the Táng, tea would henceforth be called *chá*. Something this special needed to be re-branded with its own character. As I mentioned in part one, the Chinese character for chá was the same as the character tú but with a single horizontal stroke removed.

09:25 The perfection of this character chá is obvious to etymologists. The top portion of the character chá has a grass radical. There's a rén, a person in the middle and a tree below. Three elements. A person in between grass and a tree. The harmony between humans and nature represented in the character *chá*.

09:50 Along with the Buddhism that spread regionally during the Suí and Táng came tea and Chinese tea culture. The people of Korea and Japan studied everything that Chinese tea and tea culture had to offer. Then each of those two unique and exquisite places did that thing that they each did to unite it with their own culture. The Táng era was the time when tea also arrived in Korea and Japan.

10:17 In the last episode, Tribute Teas or gòngchá were mentioned. These were teas considered special and extraordinary in their uniqueness and flavor. And the finest tasting leaves and buds of the most prized teas, the cream of the harvest, the earliest buds plucked before the Qīngmíng Festival in early April, these were reserved solely for the emperor. Everything that was harvested after that was for everyone else. The number of tribute teas in the Táng grew and some of them are still around today.

THE TEA HISTORY PODCAST BOOK 1
PART 3

10:48 | Let's take a look at how tea makers in the Táng Dynasty made their tea. They picked their tea leaves early in the morning, preferably when the dew was still moist on the leaf. The leaves would be boiled in a pot to prevent oxidation and to preserve the green color but at the same time get rid of the grassy smell.

11:08 | The boiled leaves would then be put in a kind of mortar and they'd be ground down to break them down a bit and force that tea sap to be released to the surface. Then the tea was put in any number of molds and was patted down to get it into a certain shape. After it was molded they would just pop it in the oven to seal in the freshness. This is how they made those tea bricks.

11:33 | And these bricks were very convenient to transport, no matter to the lower reaches of the Yangzi River or over the mountains to Tibet. If the tea was going to Tibet, Qīnghǎi, Xīnjiāng or Mongolia it was known as *biānchá* or Border Tea, tea that was sold to the border regions. The quality standards were, as I just said, much lower than what was demanded inside China.

11:58 | Let's talk more about why tea was so critical to these Tibetan, Qiāng and other minority peoples rimming China. As I said, the mountains of the Himalayas wasn't a good climate to plant gardens or engage in agriculture. The Tibetan diet had always been reliant mostly on meat; yaks and goats. This mostly meat diet had always exposed them to any number of health problems related to nutrition.

12:24 You wouldn't expect that a beverage like tea is filled with so many nutrients. Drinking it like they did, with butter, salt and sometimes other additives, was like popping vitamins.

12:35 Tea has vitamins C, D, K and E. It has fluoride, manganese, potassium, chromium, calcium, magnesium, iron, copper, zinc and other nutrients. The mineral content has a lot to do with the water you're using too. And there's more fluoride in your tea than in the water supply piped in to your residence. There's also carotene, B1, B2, B6, folic acid. Tea doesn't have everything and doesn't contain 100% of the minimum daily requirements, but in the case of the Tibetans and these other border peoples, five to six cups of tea a day gave them about 75% of what was required. It was many times better than nothing.

13:20 I'm sure everyone has seen or heard of these medical studies that claim tea prevents cancer, heart disease and diabetes. There are weight loss teas touted all over the place. Claims are made on TV, in the markets, magazines and in the health food world and all over the internet. And the world of the bǎojiànpǐn. Health products. Some teas are said to help lower cholesterol. Some aid in digestion. I don't want to get too deep into this aspect of tea, but I'm sure many of you are aware that this market segment does exist.

13:56 I guess the most important aspect of tea that is always pointed to as THE most important health benefit concerns flavonoids. These antioxidants are said to be particularly helpful in fighting cancer, heart disease,

THE TEA HISTORY PODCAST BOOK 1
PART 3

	Alzheimer's and clogged arteries by attacking what's known as free radicals inside your body that might trigger a cancer problem. Free radicals are also known to cause aging and heart disease as well.
14:24	Of the Six Classes of Tea, green, yellow, white, black, oolong and Pŭ-Ěrh, each one has their own particular merits as far as what studies have found. The different teas have different polyphenol counts. The polyphenols are the anti-oxidants that neutralize free radicals and whose amazing merits are splashed all over these health drink labels and fruit drinks.
14:51	If you can't keep all the marketing straight, tea or white and green tea in particular, are praised as antioxidants. There are studies that claim green tea lowers total cholesterol and raises HDL cholesterol, a.k.a. the good one. Others swear by green tea as a preventative against bladder, breast, ovarian, colorectal, esophageal, lung, pancreatic, prostate, skin and stomach cancers. And also as an aid in preventing Crohn's Disease and diabetes. As I said, the antioxidants in tea are called polyphenols or natural phenols. The polyphenols in tea are classified as catechins. You'll see these words in all kinds of ads and packaging on everything from tea leaves, tea extracts and other dietary supplements.
15:42	Green tea contains six primary catechin compounds called EGCG. EGCG is the most studied of the polyphenols. White tea has the highest level of antioxidants and an amino acid, discovered in 1949, called theanine. A lot of people take theanine supplements to prevent diseases

THE TEA HISTORY PODCAST BOOK 1
PART 3

like Alzheimer's and hypertension. In short, tea is healthy for you but arguments abound about how to reliably and accurately measure the exact benefits to your health and longevity.

16:19 Anyway, back to the history. Once this great market was built in Tibet, transport links had to be established. This was easier said than done because once you start heading due west from Chengdu towards Tibet it doesn't take long before you hit the Himalayas. Back in the days of Zhāng Qiān and the earliest years of the Silk Road in the Hàn Dynasty it took a bit of time to figure out the right mountain passes to traverse and where and what time of year to cross certain rivers and how to safely get from point A to point B.

16:53 For the Ancient Tea-Horse Route, the same held true. It took some time before these traders and caravan leaders got it down to a system. It was a treacherous journey across the most rugged terrain in all of China. Five-thousand-meter mountain passes, valleys and gorges. Some rivers were impassable and required cables to be run from side to side and all people, cargo and animals too, had to be zip-lined across.

17:24 Part of these caravan routes through the mountains were called Shǔ yǔ niǎo zhī lù, The road of mice and birds. This meant the paths that were carved into the mountainsides were so narrow as they wound through these these gorges, there was only sufficient room for either a mouse or a bird to walk safely.

THE TEA HISTORY PODCAST BOOK 1
PART 3

17:43 | This whole border trade industry was promoted by the government. China had tea and the Tibetans and other border people had horses. The Tang and later the Sòng government could never get enough horses in their stables. Táng Tàizōng had really pushed the limits of the empire out as far as they had ever been. In order to patrol an empire this big you needed a lot of horses. West of China they had an ample supply and were only too anxious to trade them for tea. The government started building their own tea plantations, especially around Sichuan. They got into the business too.

18:19 | As the story goes it was in the year 641 that tea first came calling on the high altitude world of the Tibetans. This is the story of Princess Wénchéng. Wénchéng Gōngzhǔ. She was Táng Tàizōng's niece. In 641 her uncle the emperor, married her off to the Tibetan king Songtsän Gampo. This was done in the interests of bringing peace and stability between China and Tibet. These two went at it for almost the entirety of the Tang Dynasty....and though it's hard to believe today, the Tibetan Empire, which lasted 618-842, really beat up on the Tang.

19:00 | Princess Wénchéng is credited with introducing Buddhism to Tibet as well as all kinds of other practical wisdom from China that had beneficial applications to the Tibetans. She also brought tea with her from Sichuan. And the Tibetans really took to it in a big way. So much so that Tibet became a whole new market for China's tea producers. And again, because the Tibetans mixed the tea with butter and spices, the demands on tea quality and subtleness of flavor weren't as important. The tea

THE TEA HISTORY PODCAST BOOK 1
PART 3

19:40 makers in Sichuan and Yunnan just churned these cakes and bricks out.

19:40 There's an old story. Who knows how much of this is true? When Princess Wénchéng was getting acclimated to the life in Lhasa, she would drink half a cup of the local milk at breakfast and chase that down with some tea to get rid of the flavor. Then she tried mixing the milk with the tea and added some clarified butter and pine nuts. And then you guessed it. She invented sūyóuchá or the famous Tibetan yak butter tea.

20:05 And from this beginning, with the union of Wénchéng Gōngzhǔ to one of the greatest kings in Tibetan history, Songtsän Gampo, not only did peace prevail between China and Tibet, the two civilizations joined together in their common embrace of Buddhism and the incorporation of tea into their daily life.

20:26 The Ancient Tea-Horse Road. In some ways this was similar to the Silk Road far to the north. It was a trade route. There were two main ones. One led from Kunming to Tibet. The other linked Chengdu straight west to Tibet. The Kunming route was called the southern route and the product was known as Southern Route Tea. It passed through the tea marketplace of Pu-Erh where it ended up being molded into bricks and sold to the Tibetans to the west. As I said already, this tea was known as biānchá or Border Tea.

21:01 Let me read from English explorer William Moorcroft. He trekked from the mouth of the Ganges to Tibet in

THE TEA HISTORY PODCAST BOOK 1
PART 3

1812. He had a fascinating observation about how the local Tibetans had their tea:

21:14

"At breakfast each person drinks about five to ten cups each containing about one-third of a pint; and when the last half is finished, he mixes with the remainder enough barley meal to bring it to the consistency of a paste. This is done to soak up and render edible a greasy accumulation of froth which is blown aside when the preceding cups are being drunk.

21:37

The preparation of breakfast tea for say, ten persons, involves boiling an ounce of brick tea and a like quantity of soda in a quart of water for an hour, or until the leaves of the tea have been sufficiently steeped. The liquid then is strained and mixed with ten quarts of boiling water in which an ounce and a half of fossil salt has been dissolved. The whole is put into a narrow, cylindrical churn, along with some butter, and is churned until it becomes a smooth, oily, brown liquid, somewhat like chocolate. In this form it is transferred to a teapot for immediate use.

22:14

At midday meal those who can afford it take tea again with wheaten cakes, accompanied by some paste of wheat flour, butter and sugar, served hot."

22:25

From Chengdu and the towns outside of Chengdu like Qiónglái, Yǎ'ān, Wènchuān, Lúshān, tea was packed up and sent out west to Tibet and northwest to Qīnghǎi and Gānsù. Once it got as far as Gānsù, you were hooked up with the Silk Road and your stuff could go anywhere

THE TEA HISTORY PODCAST BOOK 1
PART 3

22:48 — in the known world where a Central Asian or Mongol trader might take it.

Now, this brick tea, although it was the accepted standard in Tang days, by the Song dynasty they're going to be turning their nose up at this stuff. In fact, interestingly enough, after the Song, the only ones besides the Tibetans who were sticking with brick tea were the Russians.

23:07 — Lù Yǔ is at stage left right now looking at his watch. As far as tea is concerned, he's really the big star of the Tang Dynasty and we've talked about everything except him. So next episode we're going to look at his life, his great work, the Chá Jīng, the Classic of Tea and the legacy that would have all the way into our present day. I haven't walked into a single teashop or tea person's home or office who didn't have at least a small Lu Yu figurine on the shelf. That's all for Part 4.

23:41 — So be sure to come back next time for the Lu Yu episode. This is Laszlo Montgomery, signing off from Los Angeles in the Golden State.

23:49 — Please consider coming back for more in two weeks time. You could do a lot worse than this niche program that's fighting its way up the pop charts. I'll be waiting for you here, the kettle boiling, for another delectable episode of the Tea History Podcast.

The Tea History Podcast
Book 1 Part 4

SUMMARY

In this episode, we finally introduce the Tea Saint. What Elvis was to rock n' roll, Lu Yu was to the popularity of tea in Chinese society. Here we'll look at his life and his celebrated work, "The Classic of Tea". From here on out, tea is no longer tú, and neither is it bitter.

TRANSCRIPT

00:00 | Hey everyone, Laszlo Montgomery again, History of Tea Part 4 today with a special focus on the Tang dynasty luminary, Lù Yǔ. I was a little reluctant to mix Lù Yǔ in with the last episode and wanted to showcase his life and the Chá Jīng, the Classic of Tea, in one single episode, namely, this one.

00:20 | I won't say that Lù Yǔ's life was as legendary and mythic as Shén Nóng. But it was twelve centuries ago when Lù Yǔ walked this earth. So it's one of those things. Who knows how much, if any of his tale, is true.

00:34 | So without further ado, let's get into it. All my sources said he was a Húběi rén. Born 733 in what is present day Tiānmén, Húběi province, between Wǔhàn and Jīngmén. Like with many of today's places in China, back in Lù Yǔ's day it wasn't called by its present name. He was

 THE TEA HISTORY PODCAST BOOK 1
PART 4

	abandoned as a child and left under a stone bridge and he ended up growing up under the care of the abbot of Lónggài Temple.
01:01	The abbot Zhi Ji raised him as his son and together with others inside the monastery served as Lù Yǔ's tea mentors for all those earliest formative years. The roots of Lù Yǔ's passion for tea were planted here at this Chán Buddhist monastery. I mentioned earlier that Chán Buddhism is better known by its Japanese name, Zen. The way the script was written by his stepfather, Lù Yǔ was supposed to stick with the monastery and embrace the life of a monk. But Lù Yǔ had other plans in mind.
01:37	The abbot's problems began after he had placed Lù Yǔ in the care of a family who taught him classical learning: Confucian values and philosophy. Lù Yǔ favored this much more than Buddhism. No matter how hard Lù Yǔ's father, the abbot, tried to push him towards Buddhism and away from Confucian learning, he just couldn't do it.
01:58	To compel Lù Yǔ to toe the line and to embrace Buddhism, Lù Yǔ's stepfather used forceful ways, punishing him by making him do all the most menial and degrading of tasks in the monastery. So fourteen-year-old Lù Yǔ, after saying 'enough of this,' ran away. He picked up and left, joined the circus and became a clown.
02:21	But being a circus performer wasn't the life for Lu Yu any more than it was for Moishe Cohen back in 1907. So Lù Yǔ didn't last long in the entertainment industry.

48

THE TEA HISTORY PODCAST BOOK 1
PART 4

02:33 | However, being in the entertainment business did have some perks. You never know what kind of interesting people and role models you might run into. Lù Yǔ received a good education in the circus. He was a natural man of letters too and of course, tended to prefer to gravitate towards people who were also literate and learned.

02:54 | A member of the Táng royal family, Lǐ Qíwù, for one insubordination or another, got banished to Tiānmén as the new governor. Tiānmén wasn't considered a prestigious posting, at that time of the Tang anyway. Despite his banishment, Lǐ Qíwù put on his best face and went down there. Of course, he sought out the local entertainment and wouldn't you know it, so enamored was he with Lù Yǔ's performing skills when he visited the circus, he sought him out for further conversation.

03:30 | This Tang royal Lǐ Qíwù then took Lù Yǔ under his wing and provided him with mentorship and the use of his library to further his studies.

03:41 | The period growing up in the monastery until the time he began writing the Chá Jīng were Lù Yǔ's most formative years. Not only did Lǐ Qíwù guide him at a crucial time in his life, others too, Zōu Fūzǐ and Cuī Guófǔ, served as Lú Yu's other teachers. These two were other respected Tang men of letters, one a teacher, the other a poet and calligrapher.

04:06 | Lù Yǔ became a man of letters himself, and in no time at all could hold his own against all the gifted literati of

THE TEA HISTORY PODCAST BOOK 1
PART 4

04:26 the day. He had built up a modicum of high repute for his writing and for being as William Ukers described, "a colorful personality of high abilities and versatility".

04:26 Lù Yǔ spent his twenties traveling far and wide to thirty-two tea-producing districts in China. This stretched from the region west of the Chéngdū basin in Sichuan all the way to 8th century tea heaven, Jiangsu, Zhejiang and Jiangxi. And all along the way he had collected samples, talked to the locals, compared processes and noted everything he saw.

04:53 During his travels, Lù Yǔ had wandered down to the land of Bā. Remember the Bā Shǔ states, centered around Chengdu and Chongqing. Tea Part 1? This is considered the birthplace of tea cultivation. Lù Yǔ studied this place and took notes wherever he went. He found solace at Miaoxi Monastery in Huzhou, Zhejiang Province. There he worked alongside the *chanong* or tea farmers working on the hillsides, and he befriended a Chan Buddhist monk named Jiǎo Rán. Jiǎo Rán was famous for his tea poems.

05:28 Jiǎo Rán, Lǐ Qíwù, Zōu Fūzǐ, Cuī Guófǔ. They all had an impact on Lù Yǔ's education and literary prowess. And by this time in the Táng, the world of letters and learning went hand in hand with tea culture and knowing how to enjoy it. Exposure to all these tea people who knew so much about tea was the stuff that gave Lù Yǔ the chops to authoritatively write something like the Classic of Tea.

05:56 | This monk Jiǎo Rán, was said to have been another one of Lù Yǔ's main mentors in the arts of preparing tea, serving it and all about the importance of the tea ware. Jiǎo Rán was in many ways the one who was the guiding spirit behind Lù Yǔ when he began writing the Chá Jīng.

06:16 | As the story goes, the reason Lù Yǔ wrote the Chá Jīng was because he had received a commission from some tea merchants. These men in the tea business, who knows if it was a guild or how this group came together. They thought it would be good for everyone if they could put out an easy to read, simple, all-inclusive guidebook to everything one needed to know about tea. That's what the Chá Jīng, the Classic of Tea, was all about. It was a written as an 8th century infomercial on behalf of the tea industry.

06:49 | So far, in examining the history of tea we have looked at all these various documents going back to that contract from Wáng Bāo where in 59 BCE tea and a tea market were specifically mentioned. For hundreds and hundreds of years as tea use in China developed, there would be references made to tea that gave an indication about where tea was, as a beverage, a medicine or a muse, at that time.

07:18 | To get an idea about how tea culture was progressing, historians have had to sift through all the documents to study this and that document that mentioned tea. But up to the time of the Táng, there was still no all-in-one guidebook that spelled it all out succinctly.

# THE TEA HISTORY PODCAST BOOK 1
PART 4

07:38 And now with Lù Yǔ's Chá Jīng, The Classic of Tea, here for the first time everything about tea was contained in one slender volume written for both experts and novices. And because of his writing skills that he had acquired growing up these past years with some pretty smart people, it was written as elegantly as it was simple.

08:01 Lù Yǔ was perfectly suited to perform this task. He was at a stage in his life where he was a brilliant mind looking for some meaning in life and to strike out and make a difference. This commission from these tea merchants turned out to be the perfect opportunity to write something he was eminently qualified to do and at the same time leave his mark in China.

08:25 His accumulated learning and passion for tea from his early days at Lónggài Monastery, his Daoist and Buddhist core values and beliefs, his skill as a literatus acquired during his patronage by Lǐ Qíwù, his travels and the times he lived in, everything combined together in Lù Yǔ's person to give us the Chá Jīng.

08:48 In 765, this was during the unstable reign of the Táng Dàizōng Emperor, he had the first draft of the Chá Jīng ready for release to these merchants. But Lù Yǔ believed the Chá Jīng wasn't complete yet and something was still missing. So in 766 a deal was reached with his sponsors to release the work in its present unfinished form but in a limited run. In all, it would take Lù Yǔ a good twenty-six years to complete the Classic of Tea in its final form.

THE TEA HISTORY PODCAST BOOK 1
PART 4

09:23 Through his old acquaintance, the Buddhist monk Jiǎo Rán, Lù Yǔ hooked up with a noted Táng official, calligrapher and all around literatus extraordinaire named Yán Zhēnqīng, around 777 CE. Yán Zhēnqīng was compiling books and documents for an imperial library for the Dàizōng emperor. Lù Yǔ was one of the many scholars invited to participate in this project and to examine and study first hand, all these ancient documents that needed categorizing.

09:57 It was during this scholarly endeavor, pouring over these scrolls, that Lù Yǔ learned for the first time all the forgotten tea history going back to Shén Nóng's time. All of this was new to Lù Yǔ and in reading about tea in the Suí, the Southern & Northern Dynasties period, the Jìn, the Three Kingdoms, Hàn and even as far back as the Zhōu, Lù Yǔ noted everything.

10:22 Acquiring all this new information, he felt at last, he had everything he needed to complete the work he had left unfinished for more than a decade going back to the year 766. Under Yán Zhēnqīng's generosity and hospitality, Lù Yǔ returned to the Chá Jīng and finished it off, inserting all the history of tea into the work.

10:44 On behalf of the Dàizōng emperor, Yán Zhēnqīng tried to recruit Lù Yǔ into government but Lù Yǔ, who had already returned to the south, would have nothing of it. He was the sort that liked to be out in nature enjoying tea rather than living a life in a cubicle at the royal palace. Nonetheless he took the return trip north to Cháng'ān to thank Yán Zhēnqīng personally for recommending him

THE TEA HISTORY PODCAST BOOK 1
PART 4

to the emperor like he did.

11:11 En route, Lù Yǔ turned this sojourn into another tea vacation. He stopped along the way at any tea-worthy village or garden, and wherever there was a mountain stream whose water was said by the locals to be regarded in high repute, Lù Yǔ would go there too. His alleged expertise in being able to recognize water purity is all part of the whole Lù Yǔ legend.

11:37 He kept finishing and polishing the Chá Jīng during this time, the late 770's. Then by the year 780, it was in its final form. By Chinese reckoning this was the year 3478, the year of the Metal Monkey. This was the year work began on Borobudur, the largest Buddhist temple in the world, located in Central Java. Man, Buddhism was big in the 8th and 9th centuries.

12:05 So, 780, the Chá Jīng, the Classic of Tea was released to the Táng general public. Everything about tea, the water, utensils, was categorized, listed, explained, and recommended with anecdotes. The impact this manual had on Chinese tea society provided instant benefits to the people who used it.

12:28 The Chá Jīng, when it came out, needless to say was an instant classic. There was no sad or tragic story about Lù Yǔ. He became an instant celebrity and was even sought out by the Táng Emperor Dézōng. Lù Yǔ lived on for another twenty-four years beyond the publication of the Cha Jing in 780. He lived to see paintings of himself and Lù Yǔ statuettes placed in teashops and tea houses throughout the land.

12:57 Lù Yǔ would later produce much more than the Chá Jīng as far as his whole body of work but like so much from this age, not too much has survived the ravages of man and nature. But we did get the Chá Jīng, so we should be thankful for that. Like so many documents from these times, no copies of the original work survived.

13:20 The Chá Jīng was a complete primer on tea culture. It touched on the horticultural aspects, plucking, processing, the tools, everything, all in one slender volume. Actually back then it came in three volumes and ten parts. But these were scrolls and not bound like books we know in our wild and crazy times. But it was indeed slender, only 7,000 Chinese characters long.

13:45 Lù Yǔ's Chá Jīng created quite a revolution in China as far as tea culture and the whole integration of tea into Chinese daily life.

13:55 In order for the tea supply to keep up with the growing national demand, tea farmers had to migrate closer to the population centers in the east. Down river along the Yángzǐ, wherever the growing conditions were right, new tea cultivation began, with Buddhists and Daoists usually leading the way. From seed planting to plucking, it only took three years. So the ramp-up phase of any tea garden venture was relatively quite fast.

THE TEA HISTORY PODCAST BOOK 1
PART 4

14:24 The Chá Jīng remained a stalwart in every educated person's library for 955 years. It wasn't until 1735, the final year of the hard working Qīng emperor Yōngzhèng, that Lù Tíngcàn, another Chá Xiān, or Tea Immortal wrote the follow-up to the Cha Jing and brought everything Lù Yǔ had written in the brick tea world of the Tang Dynasty up to date. A lot had happened between 780 and 1735. This supplement to the Cha Jing, called the Xù Chá Jīng was a long time coming. Xù Chá Jīng simply means the Sequel to the Cha Jing.

15:06 There were countless other treatises on tea and tea culture that came out or had been alluded to in other texts. We'll mention others as we make our way through the Tea History Podcast. But many of the older texts suffer from "Xià Dynasty syndrome". We heard of them. They're written about but none of these documents exist in any collections, public or private. There's no real historical evidence to prove many of these documents' existence or what information they contained.

15:36 As short and skinny as the Cha Jing was, it had a lot going on. Lu Yu didn't just offer a step by step instruction guide on to how to make tea. The spiritual aspect of tea was particularly emphasized by Lu Yu. He was insistent that serenity, oneness with nature and the universe, complete peace and focus was a necessary component of making, serving and drinking tea.

16:03 Lu Yu emphasized that the environment where you were drinking tea mattered very much. The entirety of the tea experience had to be a serene moment. The

THE TEA HISTORY PODCAST BOOK 1
PART 4

preparation, the ingredients, the water, the tea ware and the tea leaves themselves. Everything needed to be just right and in tune with one's inner harmony.

16:24 The act of making, serving and drinking tea was the outward form of all of this combined inner harmony. You achieved this inner harmony through the focus and attention you put into this act of preparing and serving tea. Inner peace can be achieved through focusing on the seemingly mundane and its importance in what you are doing at that specific moment.

16:47 Lù Tíngcàn's work followed a similar structure to Lu Yu but by his time, in the Qing, it was already a loose tea world and in Lu Yu's day they were still scraping bricks of tea.

17:00 By the way, Lù Tíngcàn and Lu Yu, though sharing a common surname, were not related. His "Sequel to the Classic of Tea", the Xù Chá Jīng was a much longer book. In addition to bringing Lu Yu up to date, it also provided commentaries on all the various tea treatises since the Tang. And we'll look at many of them in the episodes to come.

17:23 So, all the rituals involved in the process were codified and a reason was given for everything. Lu Yu borrowed from both Confucianism and Daoism in producing this work. For this work and his personal contribution to Zhongguo cha wenhua, Chinese tea culture, he's forever referred to as the Cha Sheng or the Tea Saint or Tea Sage. He is also considered as the first apostle of tea in China.

 THE TEA HISTORY PODCAST BOOK 1
PART 4

17:53 | Next episode, in Part 5, we are going to take a look at the Classic of Tea and peruse these chapters written twelve and a half centuries before. I guarantee you this is one you will not want to miss.

18:04 | So let's put the bookmark in here and finish up with the Tea Saint in the next episode.

18:09 | Before I go, let me insert one shameless plug here to cajole all of you to go check out the China History Podcast, the longest running show of its kind on the internet. There's more to Chinese history than tea, and I cordially invite you to go check it out. It's available in all the same places you can find this show.

18:28 | So until the next time, Mis amigos y amigas, this is Laszlo Montgomery wishing you all a fond adieu and entreating you to consider coming back next time for what's shaping up to be another Lu-Yu-riffic episode of the Tea History Podcast.

The Tea History Podcast
Book 1 Part 5

SUMMARY

We looked at Lu Yu in the last episode. This time, we give a once-over to his masterpiece, The Cha Jing or Classic of Tea. The national popularity of tea in China really catches fire after Lu Yu shows everyone how to enjoy it, and enjoy life at the same time.

TRANSCRIPT

00:00 Welcome back everyone. Laszlo Montgomery here with the Tea History Podcast. Part 5 already. So sorry to leave you all hanging like I did, telling you everything you wanted to know about the Tea Saint Lù Yǔ but were afraid to ask. And then when we got to the best part, the actual Classic of Tea, the Chá Jīng, I abruptly ended the episode.

00:21 But wait no more. Let's now open up the Classic of Tea and see what Lu Yu had to say. For the Cha Jing there are no shortage of sources all over the place. I used what I thought was a good one. It was entitled "The Classic of Tea, Origins and Rituals" translated and introduced by Francis Ross Carpenter. That came out on Ecco Press in 1974. That's the one I recommend.

THE TEA HISTORY PODCAST BOOK 1
PART 5

00:47 | Let's just go through the ten chapters that make up the Cha Jing and if there are any noteworthy quotes from Lu Yu, I'll read from Francis Ross Carpenter's translation of the Classic of Tea.

00:59 | The Confucianist in Lu Yu led him to present the Cha Jing in a very organized, methodical way, using lists and precise steps to explain everything.

01:10 | Lu Yu said, "To quench our thirst, we drink boiled water. To expel anxiety or melancholy, we drink wine. To clear our heads, we drink tea."

01:24 | Chapter one gives all the history, horticulture, growing conditions, when to pluck and how everything affects the tea. Let me quote,

01:32 | *"In planting and transplanting tea, the same techniques apply as for a melon, but the tea may not be picked until the plant's third year. Tea that grows wild is superior; garden tea takes second place. Whether grown on sunny slopes or in shady groves, the best leaves are russet. These are superior to the green leaves. Tea from the young tender shoots in a plant's first flush is better than that from the buds. The best leaves are those that are tightly curled. Leaves that are open and unrolled are of second quality. Tea picked on the slopes or in the valleys of a sunless mountainside is not worth the effort."*

02:16 | With respect to some of tea's health benefits let me quote again:

THE TEA HISTORY PODCAST BOOK 1
PART 5

02:20 | "If one is generally moderate but is feeling hot or warm, given to melancholia, suffering from aching of the brain, smarting of the eyes, troubled in the four limbs or afflicted in the hundred joints, he may take tea four or five times. Its liquor is like the sweetest dew of Heaven."

02:41 | The tea liquid, in the biz that is, amongst the cognoscenti baby, known as the liquor. In evaluating tea, one looks not only at the taste and smell but the color of the liquor.

02:54 | After a lifetime of associating the word liquor to distilled spirits, it was hard for me to overcome the other definition of liquor as a liquid produced in a process of some kind.

03:05 | Chapter two is all about the tools of the trade. Lu Yu listed the fifteen utensils you had to have back in his day. Fifteen tools required to correctly carry out all the tasks involved in the plucking of tea, steaming, molding and all the steps needed to ensure the tea brick was properly sealed and storage-ready. He names a basket, furnace and cauldron, boiler, pestle, shaper, holder and so on down the line. If you were looking to make tea, you needed these fifteen things.

03:42 | Regarding the manufacture of tea, Lu Yu says in Chapter 3:

03:47 | "Tea is picked in the second, third and fourth moons. Young and tender shoots, growing on rich, fertile soil, should not be pulled until they look like fern or bracken and are four to five inches long. In any case, the shoots should be picked only while the dew is still cool."

THE TEA HISTORY PODCAST BOOK 1
PART 5

04:04 | "Do not pick on the day that has seen rain or when clouds spoil the sky. Pick tea only on a clear day. All there is to making tea is to pick it, steam it, pound it, shape it, dry it, tie it and seal it."

04:24 | Hey, nuff said, no wonder so many people got into the tea business.

04:27 | Also from chapter 3, Francis Ross Carpenter's translation:

04:31 | "Among would-be connoisseurs, there are those who praise the excellence of a tea by noting its smoothness and commenting upon the gloss jet shades of the liquor. They are the least capable judges. Others will tell you it is good because it is yellow, wrinkled and has depressions and mounds. They are better judges. But the really superior taster will judge tea in all its characteristics and comment upon both the good and the bad."

05:02 | Chapter 4 concerns the Équipage. That's a $64 word meaning the equipment for a particular purpose, which in this case is the storing, preparation and serving of tea. Lu Yu listed twenty-four must-have items in a complete tea set. And the cool thing was, the 24th item was a carryall case like those Asprey picnic sets. Lu Yu's all-in-one solution.

05:29 | Chapter 5 Lu Yu elucidates on the fine points of making your own tea. As I said Lu Yu's expertise in water was legendary. He said about this subject:

THE TEA HISTORY PODCAST BOOK 1
PART 5

05:41 "On the question of what water to use, I would suggest that tea made from mountain streams is best, river water is all right, but well-water is quite inferior. Water from the slow-flowing stream, the stone-lined pools or milk-pure springs is the best of mountain water. Never take tea made from water that falls in cascades, gushes from springs, rushes in a torrent or that eddies and surges as if nature were rinsing its mouth. Over usage of all such water to make tea will lead to illnesses of the throat."

06:16 Not all teas require the same temperature of water to steep the leaves. If you use the same water temperature for some delicate white or green tea as you would for Assam tea you'll really do the tea a disservice. But without a handy thermometer around, how did you measure the water temperature? A standard needed to be established to describe the temperature of the water as it progressed to a full boil. Lu Yu famously put it this way,

06:44 "When the water is boiling, it must look like fishes' eyes and give off but a hint of sound. When at the edges it chatters like a bubbling spring and looks like pearls innumerable strung together, it has reached the second stage. When it leaps like breakers majestic and resounds like a swelling wave, it is at its peak. Any more and the water will be boiled out and should not be used."

07:11 And adding his two cents to what the Ěr Yǎ said, Lu Yu himself remarked:

THE TEA HISTORY PODCAST BOOK 1
PART 5

07:16 | "When tea has a sweet flavor, it may be called jiǎ. If it is less than sweet and of a bitter or strong taste, it is called chuǎn. If it is bitter or strong when sipped but sweet when swallowed, it is called cha."

07:30 | Chapter 6 is pretty important. This is where Lu Yu generously offers up some wisdom and advice on drinking tea. He also traces the history of tea since Shén Nóng. In this chapter, Lu Yu lets loose about adding stuff to your tea. If you recall going back to the earliest days of tea this had been a common practice going back to the Bā-Shǔ days in ancient Sichuan. Lu Yu had this to say about that:

07:59 | "Sometimes such items as onion, ginger jujube fruit, orange peel, dogwood berries or peppermint are boiled along with the tea. Such ingredients may be merely scattered across the top for glossy effect, or they can be boiled together and the froth drawn off. Drinks like that are no more than the swill of gutters and ditches; alas, it is a common practice to make tea this way."

08:25 | Chapter 7 concerns the gallery of famous people who drank tea. Lu Yu reaches back in history all the way to Shén Nóng of course. He insisted it all began with him. Following Shén Nóng as worthy imbibers of tea were such luminaries as the Duke of Zhōu, Zhōu Gōng.

08:42 | Lu Yu went back through history and gave reference after reference concerning various greats and near greats from the Zhōu, Hàn, Jìn all the way up till his time. He offers up a slew of vignettes and tea stories from various

THE TEA HISTORY PODCAST BOOK 1
PART 5

surviving documents through the ages. This is most likely the information he picked up when he was up in Cháng'ān working for Yán Zhēnqīng on that imperial library project.

09:08 Chapter 8 is just a listing of all the various tea producing areas all over China at that time as well as the kinds of tea produced there and its quality ranking.

09:19 In Chapter 9 Lu Yu gives you all the minutiae involving what tools or utensils can be excluded under certain conditions. He really gets down in the details here and tries to think of everything that might happen to someone in the late 8th century and how to deal with it, as far as making tea was concerned.

09:40 One thing the Tea Sage was adamant about is that if optimal conditions exist and there is nothing that is out of order, you had better have all twenty-four things that he enumerates in Chapter 4. In fact Lu Yu simply says, "If one of the twenty-four implements is missing in an aristocratic family living inside the city, then tea cannot be prepared."

10:06 Chapter 10 I'll just read the whole thing cause it's very short. Here Lu Yu tells everyone how to take the Cha Jing and re-do it onto scrolls that can be hung on the wall of any teahouse or scholar's residence for instant reference.

10:21 As I said, the impetus to produce the Cha Jing were certain powers in the tea business who believed a manual on everything one needed to know about tea

THE TEA HISTORY PODCAST BOOK 1
PART 5

would benefit both vendors and customers. So this final chapter was meant to guide teashops how to properly display the Cha Jing in their fine establishment. The great tea saint said:

10:44 "On white silk of four or six rolls, copy it so that it can be hung in sections. Spread the sections out in order in the corner of the room where the seats would be. Arrange them so that "The Beginnings of Tea," "The Tools of Tea," "The Manufacture of Tea," "The Équipage," "The Brewing of Tea," "Drinking the Tea," "Notations on Tea," Tea-Producing Areas" and "Generalities" can be taken in at a glance and retained in memory."

11:14 Again, "The Classic of Tea, Origins and Rituals," Translated and Introduced by Francis Ross Carpenter.

11:21 In reading Lu Yu's Classic of Tea. It sounds so matter-of-fact and clinical in English. In the Classical Chinese that Lu Yu used, it was delivered in a very poetic and special way. You know, the original text of the Cha Jing, as Lu Yu exactly wrote it, was lost. Surprise, surprise. It resurfaced in the Ming Dynasty during the Hongzhi era as part of a larger compendium of work. The Hóngzhì Emperor was about midway-ish into the dynasty. So it's uncertain if the Cha Jing we read today is the same exact version of Lu Yu's time in the mid Tang Dynasty.

12:01 After the Cha Jing was released for general circulation all over China, the whole practice of the tea ceremony and all the early tea culture was embraced by everyone who could afford to buy their own equipage.

THE TEA HISTORY PODCAST BOOK 1
PART 5

12:15 It didn't take long for the Cha Jing to make its way to Japan where it also created quite a sensation. The Emperor of Japan began demanding tribute tea as well, just like the Emperor of China got. The Japanese took the Cha Jing and injected it with their own culture and sensibilities and in doing so, produced their own unique Japanese tea ceremony that would be taken to new heights after the Sòng Dynasty.

12:41 Tea had been adopted by the Zen Buddhist monks early on and was institutionalized within the religion. The rituals they created about tea, meditation, drinking tea before images of Daruma and Sakyamuni was the seed from which the whole Japanese 'cha no yu' tea ceremony began.

13:01 What can we call Lu Yu's legacy? I guess it was the way he used plain but elegant words, to tell tea's story. One thing's for certain. He raised the status of tea from a thirst quenching beverage to something that could be savored as well as enjoyed.

13:18 Some people maintain that tea is a religion of sorts. If that's so, then Lu Yu would be the highest deity.

13:26 Lu Yu, the legend yielded many interesting and memorable stories. Let me mention a couple of the more famous. It's said that Lu Yu's stepfather, Abbot Zhìjī of Lónggài Monastery, late in life, had given up drinking tea, so upset and disappointed was he when his adopted son Lu Yu ran away a second time from Lónggài Temple. Remember he blew off the life of a monk to try his luck in the circus?

13:53 Abbot Zhìjī, after Lu Yu bolted from the monastery gave up this passion in his life and insisted no one could prepare tea like his Lu Yu. He was adamant and true to his word all these years that not unless his son Lu Yu prepared the tea could it be possible for him to ever drink tea again.

14:14 The Dézōng Emperor, upon hearing of this story decided to have a little fun and one day invited the Abbot up to Cháng'ān.

14:21 The emperor wanted to test this claim out. He arranged for his most gifted tea expert, a palace court lady, to prepare tea for Abbot Zhìjī to see if he could accept it. Not that she had any pressure on her, but she did her best and made and served tea to Abbot Zhìjī. The Abbot, not wanting to breach any etiquette, accepted the brew graciously and sipped without comment. Eh! Nothing special.

14:50 Then the Emperor Dézōng told the Abbot he had one more master preparing tea in the back room and he beseeched him to try this particular tea. Behind a screen, away from the Abbot, the emperor had arranged for Lu Yu to come to the palace in Cháng'ān and to secretly prepare tea for his estranged stepfather, Abbot Zhìjī. Lu Yu did this and the tea prepared by this mystery tea master behind the screen, was presented to the Abbot.

THE TEA HISTORY PODCAST BOOK 1
PART 5

15:22 | He took one sip and of course, you know what happens. He proclaimed it excellent and worthy and at that point Lu Yu was trotted out and they had a happy reunion right there in the palace. And the emperor was delighted that he could witness such a thing in person and to learn this legend was all true. Too bad nobody got it on video.

15:44 | The other story is a brief anecdote concerning Lu Yu's amazing ability to judge the purity of water. I've mentioned that water is the mother of tea and just pouring it out of the tap or drawing it from a well is simply not going to pass muster with the tea snobs and tea experts. Water was special and Lu Yu knew his water.

16:06 | It's said that once he was enjoying a nice Yangzi River cruise one day near Yángzhōu on the boat of a Chinese general. The general told Lu Yu that the water from the nearby Nánlíng River was absolutely pure and that he had sent a few soldiers to retrieve some of this water to prepare tea for him. And the general told them sternly, make sure you draw the water from the center of the river where it was sweetest and purest.

16:32 | When they got back Lu Yu asked for a sampling of the water they had carried back. He tasted this river water that purportedly was drawn from the center of the river. He shook his head and said this water couldn't have come from the center. It tastes like it came from near the banks of the river, where it was less pure. Lu Yu's host exclaimed how could this be. He had asked his men purposely to draw the water from the center of the river. He called one of them over to explain.

THE TEA HISTORY PODCAST BOOK 1
PART 5

17:00 The frightened soldier, when confronted with this accusation, blubbered that this water came from the center of the river. Lu Yu said this water came from near the river banks at best and in no way tasted pure enough. Lu Yu had some of the water poured out and tasted from another part of the cistern and proclaimed that this bit of water seemed from the center of the river.

17:25 Upon hearing that, the soldier finally admitted that he had drawn the water from the center of the Nánlíng River as instructed but when he got near the banks of the river some of the water accidentally had spilled out. So, to avoid getting into any trouble he topped off the water cistern with water from near the river banks. See? No fooling Lu Yu. He knew.

17:47 So the Tang Dynasty, they inherited all the momentum tea had made in the Nánběi Cháo and the Suí. In the short Sui dynasty, tea had just started to become a social beverage rather than simply a medicine or health product. By the time of the last Tang emperor in the early 10th century, the practice of drinking tea will have not only permeated the entirety of China, it will have woven itself inexorably into the fabric of daily Chinese life. From the highest court rituals down to the most common, mean family, tea became a common thread joining together everyone in China.

18:30 Arab traders regularly making the Middle East-Chang'an run were writing as far back as the mid 9th century that tea was a common beverage in China. If it wasn't already, surely tea was on its way to becoming the national beverage of China.

18:47 Thanks to the great Lǐ Shìmín, the Táng Tàizōng emperor, the whole idea of reserving the best of the best for the emperor's own consumption, the tribute tea system began. And thanks to the diplomatic alliance between Tibet and China, tea was brought to that rather inaccessible place. And from this sprouted the whole Ancient Tea-Horse Road that in turn produced stories and legends known by the mountain people of Sichuan and Yunnan.

19:16 Tea got so big the government themselves felt obligated to get involved. They too got into the business of managing tea gardens, tribute and taxes. Later on, the Tang government would essentially nationalize all tea. And from the outset, Buddhists, Confucianists and Daoists would always be tea's biggest proponents and champions.

19:40 When Lu Yu came on to the scene, he essentially showed everyone how to grow tea, produce it, prepare it, and drink it. He also preached a tea philosophy that at first was embraced by the elites, aristocrats and educated classes and then a lot of others joined in as well. And this philosophy called for tea drinking to take on a central role in seeking and enjoying peace of mind and an escape from the demands of everyday life into a world where you could forget all your troubles and live in the moment. And the ambience, the tea ware and utensils all had a great impact on the outcome of the total experience.

20:22 | Regarding the whole debate about Yuè ware vs. Xíng ware debate. You remember we mentioned this from a previous episode. Lu Yu was a Yuè ware guy. He gave several reasons why the beautiful and delicate white Xíng ware from Héběi in the north, was an inferior experience compared to the greenish celadon ware from Yuèzhōu in Zhejiang. Lu Yu spelled it out that in comparing the two, Xíng ware was like silver to Yuè ware's jade. Xíng ware was snow, Yuè ware was ice. Xíng ware, with its whiteness allowed you to see the color of the tea more clearly. But only from Yuè ware did the tea have its greenish color.

21:06 | If you visit Tiānmén in Húběi today, to honor their hometown hero there's a Lu Yu Square, a Lu Yu Park, Lu Yu Avenue, Lu Yu Garden and I'm sure there's a Lu Yu Tea House somewhere. All things Lu Yu.

21:21 | And in Hong Kong of course, the Luk Yu Tea House on Stanley Street in Central. This has been a Hong Kong institution going back to 1933. I've been there several times myself, always upstairs of course and not in the downstairs part reserved only for their best guests.

21:40 | Lu Yu warned against drinking cold tea and said it gave one indigestion. From what I read, about 85% of the tea consumed in the USA is iced. What would Lu Yu have to say about that?

21:53 | So let's just put the bookmark in here. Next episode we're going to pick up in the post-Lu Yu world and see how things were after the fall of the Tang, the Five

THE TEA HISTORY PODCAST BOOK 1
PART 5

Dynasties and Ten Kingdoms period and then the Northern Song Dynasty. We'll take another look at our old friend Emperor Huīzōng again. He was a big tea drinker and proponent of all that was good about tea. All for next time.

22:17 For now this is your humble narrator Laszlo Montgomery signing off again from sunny Southern California. Once again I invite you to go check out the China History Podcast, considered by many to be one of the best China history shows out there. Take care everyone and I hope you'll consider staying with the program and consider coming back next time for another mouth-watering episode of the Tea History Podcast.

The Tea History Podcast
Book 1 Part 6

THE TRANSCRIPTS

SUMMARY

In the post-Lu Yu world, tea starts to take off like a rocket. It will take a little longer for tea to get the needed traction in Japan but during the Tang, they get to see it and appreciate it up close. We'll also look at one of the early "Tea Persons", the poet and recluse Lu Tong, as well as one of his most famous tea poems. In this episode, we also introduce the first popular tea ware, Yue ware and Xing ware.

TRANSCRIPT

00:00 Hey everyone Laszlo Montgomery here, back again with the sixth installment of this vainglorious attempt of mine at immortality, introducing the history of tea. On behalf of everyone here at the Tea History Podcast, welcome back.

00:15 We left off just as I was beginning to introduce the Chámǎ Gǔdào. The Ancient Tea Horse Road. At the exact same time that the earliest development of the Tea-Horse Road was ramping up, one of the great countries and cultures of Asia was bellying up at the bar sipping away at the delights and pleasures of Chinese culture.

00:39 For Japan, India was far too away but China was conveniently located just across the East China Sea. That's where the Japanese went to learn the customs of

THE TEA HISTORY PODCAST BOOK 1
PART 6

China, see the sights, check out the Buddhist temples and bring everything of use back to Japan where it was reverse engineered, modified to suit local tastes and sensibilities and then these threads were woven into the ever-emerging Japanese fabric.

01:09 The Japanese during the Tang Dynasty came for the Buddhism but they went back to Japan with plenty of tea also. And a few other things. But those two? Buddhism and tea? Those two valuable acquisitions came at the same time. And as I mentioned, in the case of Zen Buddhism they became one.

01:28 This wasn't the first time these two great nations and peoples got to see each other up close. China and Japan first met back in 57 CE, Eastern Hàn, the time of Emperor Guāngwǔ. But things really began to heat up during the Suí. These were the Kentoshi or Qiǎn Táng Shǐ of the 7th to 9th centuries. Between 607 to 838. Japan sent nineteen embassies to China.

01:56 Let me introduce Saichō. He came to China late in the Tang Dynasty, around 803-804 during Dézōng's reign. During his time in China, Saichō soaked up all the culture and learning that he could humanly take in. This is right at the early part of the Hei'an era during the reign of Japanese Emperor Saga, 809 to 823. And in the West, this was also the exact time Charlemagne reigned and founded the Carolingian Empire.

02:27 Saichō became a monk at the age of fourteen. He was outstanding in every way and in his twenties retreated

THE TEA HISTORY PODCAST BOOK 1
PART 6

to Mt. Hiei outside of Kyoto, to continue his Buddhist studies and devotions. He developed quite a following there and those even vaguely familiar with Japan will know Mt. Hiei is where the Enryakuji is located. One of the world's great temples, established by Saichō himself in 788.

02:56 Saichō had received a directive from no less a person than the emperor of Japan who told him to go travel around China and bring back as many Buddhist texts as possible. And while he was at it, create friendly relations with the Táng Empire too.

03:14 With regard to Buddhism, Saichō was specifically tasked with studying the Tiāntái sect of Buddhism. This is one that was purely home grown in China and didn't get transplanted from India. You've all probably heard of the famous Lotus Sutra. Well, that's associated with this particular sect. Saichō was asked to study their teachings as much as possible.

03:40 Saichō did as he was told and eight months after arriving he headed back to Tsushima on a vessel that sailed from Ningbo. Saicho brought some tea seeds back with him that he had acquired on this mission and planted them in Sakamoto Village in Omi Prefecture on the slopes of Mt. Hiei. This original tea garden is said to still exist in Ikegami.

04:02 It was right after Saichō returned from China that he made tea for Emperor Saga and received imperial support in promoting tea drinking and cultivation. Tea,

THE TEA HISTORY PODCAST BOOK 1
PART 6

as it was in its current unrefined brick form in the Táng, didn't particularly go down too well with the Japanese market or nobility. It didn't catch fire in Japan during this Tang period. But seeds were transported and trees take time to grow. Later during the Kamakura period 1185-1392, the timing and the technology of tea making would be all ready to conquer Japan. We'll talk about Eisai when we get to the Sòng period.

04:47 As we saw following the Classic of Tea, this beverage fully penetrated the mass market during the Tang. This penetration into the daily lives of most all Chinese would be even greater during the Song. But now in the 8th and 9th centuries, the word had gotten out and everybody was drinking tea. The government again saw an opportunity and created a whole arm of the administration to deal with a tea tax.

05:15 After the salt and steel tax, tea brought in the greatest amount of revenue for the Tang treasury. The Dézōng emperor tried taxing tea first unsuccessfully in 780 when Lu Yu published the Cha Jing and tea sales started to get real hot. This initial tea tax was repealed for a while due to the politics of the time not being quite right. But as soon as the time was more politically feasible, the emperor put it in place again in 793.

05:45 Tea cultivation made a lot of progress during the Tang dynasty. They figured out during the Tang that tea trees and plants love shade. This tipped farmers off to plant the tea bushes in the shadiest places along the northern slopes of the hills and mountains. As more and more knowledge about tea cultivation accumulated and with domestic and overseas demand growing like it was, it put even further incentive on farmers to leave Sichuan and begin heading east along the Yangzi River valley to plant new tea gardens there. A lot of the most legendary tea gardens out east began this way.

06:26 The manufacturing and packaging process for brick tea had been further advanced during the Tang. They came up with new ways to mold these tea bricks and make them easier to transport and stay fresh along the way. When these human pack animals of the Tang era were hauling this brick tea on their sturdy backs through the dangerous mountain passes of the Himalayas, tea still had seven centuries to go yet before European people have their first sip.

06:54 The tea culture early on was developed around the imperial court with the emperor of course at the center of it all. And after new ways to drink it in Cháng'ān, Luòyáng, Kāifēng or Běijīng were thought up, this new way of preparing the tea or serving the tea or some new aspect of tea culture, instantly became fashionable.

07:14 So you can say during the Tang, tea really went up and down market. Both the masses and the nobles for the first time in history were mutually enjoying tea. And tea as an art, as fashion, in literature, as a philosophy, all of this finally came together in the Tang. Tea had evolved into a powerful muse that inspired unknown numbers of masterpieces in art and literature that have survived throughout the ages.

THE TEA HISTORY PODCAST BOOK 1
PART 6

07:48 Also around this same time, the early 800's, there lived a man of letters named Lú Tóng. Lù Yǔ of course, is the better known of the two because of the Chá Jīng but Lú Tóng is a very close second place with his great body of work in Tang poetry in general and for his famous tea poems, most notable Qī wǎn chá or "Seven Bowls of Tea" in particular.

08:11 Lú Tóng's poem is considered the definitive Tang dynasty tea poem. Not only was it popular in China but in Japan as well. And there were a lot of tea poems that came out of that golden era. Lú Tóng was famous for many things. Writing under the pen name of Yù Chuānzǐ 玉川子, he became renowned for his poems and his love of and expertise in all things tea. He was also known for his wisdom and good sense as well as for his several eccentricities, mostly manifested in his reclusive lifestyle. All these facets of his life combined into one single human unit, made Lú Tóng quite an endearing Tang dynasty personage.

08:56 He lived this hermit-like existence out in this beautiful mountain in Henan not far from Shàolín Temple. He came from money so Lú Tóng never had to worry where his next bowl of congee was coming from. Lú Tóng lived an idyllic scholarly life in every way. He drank tea all day long and important people often came to seek his counsel.

09:18 Lú Tóng was a young man when Lu Yu's blockbuster came out. Their two lives had fourteen years of overlap when both an aged Lù Yú and a young Lú Tóng were living.

09:32 Lú Tóng was totally uncorrupted by money and politics. Despite all the attempts by government officials to recruit him he always said, that life wasn't for him. He was an ardent Dàoist and followed the Dào in all ways.

09:45 He was incorruptible. Nobody could buy him. But Lú Tóng could be tempted with the right tea. He was credited with saying, "I care not a bit for immortal life, but only for the taste of tea."

10:00 I told you the Tribute Tea system really took off during the Tang emperors. And honestly, how much could the emperor drink? So all these fantastic teas, finest in all the land, a lot of product trickled down to those who hung around the imperial palace. Lú Tóng knew one such guy and one day this person, someone who had access to the emperor himself, came calling on Lú Tóng and brought him a very special gift that had been handed to him before by the emperor himself. So he was sort of re-gifting this tea that had come direct from the emperor's own stash. And this official had now come down to the Lake Tài area in Jiangsu and was now giving this tea to Lú Tóng.

10:43 Later on in the series we'll look at many of these tribute teas. There's so many of them. But this one in particular, Yángxiàn Zǐsǔn chá, this one was not easy to get your hands on, at least not the quality that went to the imperial palace in Chang'an.

11:01 This Zǐsǔn or Purple Bamboo tea was, I read, the first true tribute tea. The operation to produce this tea began

THE TEA HISTORY PODCAST BOOK 1
PART 6

in 770, the Tang Daizong emperor's time. Yángxiàn tea came from Mount Gùzhǔ near the Lake Tai area, the famous lake in China surrounded by the cities of Sūzhōu, Húzhōu, Chángxīng, Yíxìng and Wúxī. Yángxiàn was the former name of what we know today as the city of Yíxìng. We'll talk about their tea ware later on in another episode.

11:34 This Yángxiàn tea was one of the earliest teas of the spring season to be picked. There was an old saying that went, "The hundred plants dare not bloom until the emperor had the first taste of Yángxiàn tea." The emperor sent his own people down to Jiangsu to personally oversee the harvesting, the packaging and to supervise the entire operation and ensure the integrity of the product that ultimately got transported up to Chang'an met with his satisfaction. The shipment had to arrive and be ready to drink before the Qingming holiday in early April. This wasn't just some ordinary tribute tea. When Lú Tóng copped a gander at this generous gift of Yángxiàn Zǐsǔn chá, he really was beholding the Holy Grail for any chárén *or tea person* like himself.

12:29 And not just the tea. The water too that flowed from nearby Jīnshā Spring. That too had to accompany the tea leaves. In order to extract the optimum tea drinking experience, the best and purest flavor, the finest aroma, the Yángxiàn Zǐsǔn cha had to be drunk with Jīnshā spring water.

12:51 I'm not kidding you, they filled containers with water from the Jīnshā spring and transported it all the way up

THE TEA HISTORY PODCAST BOOK 1
PART 6

to Chang'an. 62.4 lbs. per cubic foot. But if you lived in the area of Húzhōu or Yíxìng, you could have it every day.

13:08 You can buy this tea today. A lot of tea shops both brick and mortar and online sell it. I don't know about the Jīnshā water, though. The way you can buy it today doesn't look at all like it did during the Tang. As we'll see over the next episodes, tea never stopped evolving. In Lú Tóng's time, in the Tang, this tea came in small convenient compressed cakes. It wasn't found in its present loose leaf form until the Ming Dynasty.

13:37 So Lú Tóng wrote this poem. It was written in the form a letter of appreciation to his friend up in the palace who had been so kind as to give him a gift fit for an emperor. I'm sure Lú Tóng appreciated it a lot more than his majesty did. So he wrote this poem and I'll just read the most famous part, where he speaks about the seven bowls of tea he pours for himself after he has shut himself in and was all alone, in his tea version of his smoking spot. Then he enjoyed this tea. I'll read both the English translation and what Lú Tóng actually wrote.

14:10 The first bowl moistens my lips and throat
一碗喉吻潤，Yī wǎn hóu wěn rùn

The second bowl breaks my loneliness
二碗破孤悶，Èr wǎn pò gū mèn

The third bowl searches my barren entrails but to find
三碗搜枯腸，Sān wǎn sōu kū cháng

THE TEA HISTORY PODCAST BOOK 1
PART 6

Therein some five thousand scrolls;
惟有文字五千卷，Wéiyǒu wénzì wǔqiān juǎn

The fourth bowl raises a slight perspiration
四碗發輕汗，Sì wǎn fā qīng hàn

And all life's inequities pass out through my pores;
平生不平事盡向毛孔散，Píngshēng bùpíngshì jǐn xiàng máokǒng sàn

The fifth bowl purifies my flesh and bones;
五碗肌骨清，Wǔ wǎn jī gǔ qīng

The sixth bowl calls me to the immortals.
六碗通仙靈，Liù wǎn tōng xiān líng

The seventh bowl could not be drunk,
七碗吃不得也，Qī wǎn chī bùdé yě

only the breath of the cool wind raises in my sleeves.
唯覺兩腋習習清風生。Wéi jué liǎngyè xíxí qīngfēng shēng

Where is Penglai Island, Yùchuānzǐ wishes to ride on this sweet breeze and go back. 蓬萊山,在何處，玉川子乘此清風欲歸去。Pénglái shān, zài héchù, Yùchuānzǐ chéng cǐ qīngfēng yù guī qù

15:32 Lú Tóng, everyone. Yeah, tea had come a long way since the Bronze Age but it still had plenty more refinement and improvement to go yet. By Lú Tóng's time in the Tang dynasty, early 9th century, tea took on a whole new importance. Tea had reached the point in scale and economics where most everyone could afford it. Not everyone got to enjoy the same quality or drink from the same teaware, but that's the same wherever you go. Quality aside, tea had become something that everyone throughout society began to demand on a daily basis. And I'm not talking once per day either.

16:08 People will say the same or similar things about their coffee. Coffee and tea both offer great pleasures, inspiration and for many, an extra stage of rocket fuel to power them through the day or through a meeting. Everyone had access to tea. It was more dear to some than to others but it was now a part of daily life in China. And as I mentioned at the outset, the border people incorporated tea into their daily life too.

16:36 And if you had tea, no matter how poor you were, you had to have some sort of tea set to make it, pour it and drink it. Well, you just need a charcoal stove, some sort of pot and two cups. But this would hardly suffice if you were someone who drank tea as more than just a thirst quencher. You needed some tea-specific utensils to do it all up right. That's how the whole tea ware industry was created in China. And out of this necessity, of course, came great innovations that inspired other porcelain treasures.

17:08 During the Tang dynasty there was a type of porcelain ware called Yuè ware. Yuèqì. Technically it was a stoneware. It came from Yuèzhōu, hence its name. Yuèzhōu would be near present day Shàoxīng, just a little east of Hángzhōu. The earliest days of Yuè ware

 THE TEA HISTORY PODCAST BOOK 1
PART 6

go back to the Later Han. The quality and design of the ceramics coming out of those kilns reached their height during the Tang. Prior to the Tang, Yuè ware had quite a following regionally, but in the Tang it became a national brand. And I think I mentioned last episode, Lu Yu, he preferred Yue ware as well.

17:46 Yuè ware was the most common tea ware in China then. It's recognizable by its yellowish or bluish green color. There was even a color of Yuè ware, reserved for the emperor called mìsè which translates to "secret color". The recipe for this glaze was a state secret. Nothing was more precious than jade back then so this Yuè ware and its celadon glaze with its jade look to it was most prized.

18:14 You recall from that Lù Yǔ episode, the Tea Saint considered Yuè ware superior to its rival product Xíng ware. For drinking tea, Yuè ware was the old established chinaware of the masses who could afford to use chinaware. Especially by the 9th century this was already not a small number.

18:34 Xíng ware, despite its failure to win over Lù Yǔ, still took the Tang Dynasty by storm. The characteristic thing about Xíng ware was its whiteness. All white, very delicate looking, the tea looks great in the cup and you can get a better appreciation of the tea's color in Xíng ware. In choosing the color of the tea ware, it was always an important consideration that the cup provided a pleasing compliment to the color of the tea you were drinking.

THE TEA HISTORY PODCAST BOOK 1
PART 6

19:03 There are a lot of differences in a tea's color from brew to brew and leaf to leaf and Xíng ware really brought it out. This kind of porcelain was also called white ware. Xíng ware was an innovation of the north, around Hebei, in the heartland where Chinese civilization began. Yuè ware came from south, south of the Yangzi.

19:24 When Western people figure out what tea is in the 17th century, it's also going to spawn a whole global industry of porcelain ware.

19:33 I know this sounds incredible to believe but Europeans didn't figure out how to make porcelain until the early 18th century. Johann-Friedrich Böttger. His shop was in Meissen not far from Dresden.

19:45 Böttger figured out how to do it. Up until his time, when he figured it out in 1705, porcelain was right up there with silver and gold as far as precious objects went. It was called white gold. So in the time of Lu Yu and Lú Tóng, the porcelain secret was still safe for another nine centuries. And trust me when Böttger discovered how to make porcelain he kept it under wraps too, passionately so.

20:13 The opening of the Grand Canal in the Sui and other transport links caused a massive network of trade to develop. With this, tea and tea culture was able to make its way from the southwest and to the east and then to the north much more easily.

THE TEA HISTORY PODCAST BOOK 1
PART 6

20:29 The awareness of tea went in all directions. We saw Princess Wénchéng and how this marriage alliance her uncle, the Taizong emperor, made with the King of Tibet brought tea, Buddhism and Chinese culture to that part of Asia. And as a direct result of this interaction, the Chámǎ Gǔdào, the ancient Tea Horse Route, that would become so developed and institutionalized in the Song, came into being.

20:57 And countless heavy loads of brick tea were carried through these dangerous mountain passes by mules and human mules. This was a rough trade and they probably didn't have a union back then. This tea brought to Tibet and other places gave a nice boost to the nutritional well being of the Zàng, Qiāng and other ethnic peoples of the Himalayas.

21:21 And we closed with Lú Tóng, one of the great characters from the Tang Dynasty and his poem, Qī Wǎn Chá, Seven Bowls of Tea. Even though the Tang was a brick tea world, they still made some good stuff. In this episode, imperial tribute teas were also mentioned and from the introduction of Lú Tóng you can see how special and refined these teas were and still are.

21:45 Go to any online tea vendor selling China loose leaf tea. These same tribute teas are still around and you can buy them. And on a cup per cup basis, very affordable to all. So you can see from Lú Tóng's poem what tea started to mean to some people for the first time. Not just a medicine anymore. In the Tang it became the drink that we know and love in our day. Something to savor. Something to bring calm, reflection, focus and inspiration. A beverage that creates a bond between humans and nature.

22:23 Throughout the Tang, the periods of disunity, the Yuan and into the Ming, all those areas from Tibet, Qinghai, Xinjiang, Central Asia, and into Mongolia, people immediately took to tea. The dating period was very quick and went straight to marriage. Wherever tea was beheld and tasted it was always, in these lands bordering China, love at first sight.

22:48 Well, into the Ming and Qing dynasties the same thing is going to happen. Only this time it's not just the border regions surrounding China, it's the whole rest of the world. And global tea-mania will be no less great than it was in Lhasa going back to Princess Wencheng's time.

23:04 And part of this great story is that by the 17th and 18th centuries, humankind had developed much better modes of transport and logistics than the Tea Horse Road. So, I leave you with that to mull over in anticipation of episodes yet to come.

23:21 This is Laszlo Montgomery, signing off once again from Los Angeles, California cordially inviting you to consider joining me next time for another wholly satisfying episode of the Tea History Podcast.

The Tea History Podcast
Book 1 Part 7

THE TRANSCRIPTS

SUMMARY

No longer is tea a bitter brew sharing a Chinese character with the one used for a bitter vegetable. Royals, officials, scholars, and common people are enjoying tea and writing poems inspired by this beverage that has taken China by storm. We also look at one of the greatest royal patrons of tea in Chinese history, the Song Emperor Huizong.

TRANSCRIPT

00:00 | Hi Everyone, me again, Laszlo Montgomery. Welcome back to the Tea History Podcast, Part 7 today. Lù Yǔ, Lú Tóng and the Tang Dynasty are behind us now, and tea has hit the big time all over China.

00:14 | In this Part 7 episode, we'll continue looking at the history of tea in China after Lù Yǔ departed us in his earthly form in the year 804.

00:25 | In the history of tea, as it pertains to Japan that is, that was a banner year. 804 not only marks the passing of China's great tea sage, two of the more famous and important people in Japanese tea history, Kukai and Saichō, both Buddhist monks, returned to Japan from China with tea seeds and knowledge of tea cultivation and tea rituals and ceremonies. We mentioned Saichō last episode but Kukai,

THE TEA HISTORY PODCAST BOOK 1
PART 7

who didn't get a mention, was no less important. Besides all he did for Buddhism, legend has it that Kukai was also given credit for inventing katakana. That's pretty big.

01:05 The Japanese emperor at the time, Emperor Saga, quite the Sinophile according to the history books, was astounded by this new China beverage and its potential. He'll go down in Japanese tea history as the first Japanese emperor to be served tea.

01:23 From past CHP episodes, we know the Tang dynasty didn't last forever and started to break down in the 9th century, finally going down for the count in 907 after a brilliant 289-year run. From the Chámǎ Gǔdào going back to the 7th century coupled with all kinds of advances in tea processing and presentation, tea had evolved into a blockbuster hit with China's neighbors to the north, west and especially southwest. That's one of the great legacies of tea in the Tang. It was a very big regional trading item.

02:03 In the 9th and 10th centuries, sailing on the high seas was still only for the most adventurous. Among these were some fearless Arab traders engaged in China trade, sailing small cargo vessels there from the Near East.

02:19 Some of you may recall the story of the shipwreck discovered in 1998. Indonesian fishermen discovered the wreck of a 50-foot long Arab dhow called the Jewel of Muscat off Belitung Island. This is an island about halfway between Borneo and Sumatra. The wreck was dated to about 830 CE, Wénzōng Emperor's time.

THE TEA HISTORY PODCAST BOOK 1
PART 7

02:42 | The wreck contained quite a large collection of Tang Dynasty artifacts. It was called the Tang Treasure. In one single shipwreck they found gold, silver and ceramic ware from Changsha, the Dìng Kilns and Yue ware. One of the bowls was dated 826 CE. If you're ever in Singapore, this is all on display there at the Maritime Experiential Museum.

03:07 | Ding ware or Dìngcí 定瓷 came from Dìngzhōu in Hebei, halfway between Bǎodìng and Shíjiāzhuāng. Dìng ware was another very popular and in-demand ceramic ware during the Táng, Sòng and Yuán periods. Originally it was a kind of knock-off of the popular white Xíng ware from around Xíngtái, also in Hebei.

03:31 | There was a very bloody and gory bridge in between the end of the Tang and the beginning of the Song Dynasty. This period lasted from 907 to 960, fifty-three years of battles and disunity before Zhào Kuāngyìn, the last general standing, founded the Song with the capital at Kāifēng, ancient Henan province. Kāifēng was called Biàn back then.

03:56 | It was about one century since Lu Yu had died when Zhào Kuāngyìn, a.k.a. Sòng Tàizǔ, sat on the throne in Kāifēng. And he ushered in a golden age that many argue was even more golden than the preceding Tang Dynasty.

04:13 | As far as tea goes, it certainly was. I know things didn't move as fast back then as they do now but still, a lot can happen in a century, especially in a place like China. As

THE TEA HISTORY PODCAST BOOK 1
PART 7

far as tea was concerned, with so many new tea artisans getting into the game, a lot of progress had been made and a lot of new teas began hitting the market. In the Song, brick tea wasn't so cool anymore.

04:40 Bricks weren't so cool, but the whole idea of compressed tea cakes were. The Song era tea cakes would be molded and embossed with all kinds of decorative lucky symbols or Chinese characters and of course they came wrapped in all these great wood block printed papers. And they used to do this thing, as a final touch, they'd scent these beautiful tea cakes with camphor wood.

05:06 It wasn't enough just to make something worthy to be an imperial tribute tea. The way the tea was packaged was also important. So, like today's marketers, these tea masters would come up with all kinds of ways to perform that final touch, that final bit of elegance and refinement that screamed out that this tea was special. Even today, the packaging for some of these higher end gift teas is really something else. So valuable were these compressed tea cakes that they actually became a de facto secondary currency.

05:41 Besides the advances in these new molded and elegant tea cakes, perhaps one of the most defining aspects of Song tea history involved the introduction and popularity of what in Mandarin we call *mǒchá* and in Japanese Matcha. This is powdered tea, leaves that have been dried, processed and then ground down into a powder. This is how they did it in the Song. The tea, in its powdered form, was mixed with the water so that

THE TEA HISTORY PODCAST BOOK 1
PART 7

	when you drank the tea, you consumed both the water and the leaves. It's totally different from steeping the leaves in your teacup or teapot.
06:22	This is where the whisk took center stage in tea preparation. I'm sure most of you are familiar with this process, especially if you know about Japanese Chado or have seen a Japanese Cha-no yu tea ceremony. It's funny. It started in China, probably at the Song court or at least in Kaifeng. Well, maybe down in the south, who knows. But when this style of preparing and drinking powdered tea got to Japan, they really took to it. They took to it so much that even to this day matcha or tencha is still very much alive and well and remains an integral part of the Cha no yu. After the Song, mǒchá got left in the dust and the Chinese went on to bigger and better things.
07:11	This method of whisking the tea into a froth was called diǎnchá. It was much more difficult than it looked. It wasn't like pouring water on instant oatmeal. There was a whole art to it.
07:24	So let's look at some of the characters, like we did last time. In this episode let's take a look at Cài Xiāng and we'll revisit our old friend Emperor Huīzōng. Some of you might remember the four-part China History Podcast series that covered this emperor's extraordinary life.
07:43	One of the ways tea was so important was as a medium for all the Northern Song artsy-fartsy types to discuss

THE TEA HISTORY PODCAST BOOK 1
PART 7

philosophy, create poetry, paintings and ceramics. The ceremony, the rituals and the meanings behind every move became so elegant and so stylized in the time of the Song. We'll look at Song tea ware that was rather new and innovative compared to what was considered stylish in the Tang.

08:10 Song ceramics are quite regular items up for auction at all the great houses, Sotheby's, Lempertz, Christies and others. These Song vases and tea ware fetch millions. Why is that? It was because craftsmen during the Song took ceramics to new heights driven by the importance of tea and what it meant to the Chinese people from the 10th to the 12th century. More of that later.

08:38 Especially after Lu Yu, who made quite a fuss about the importance of the tea ware you used, the brilliant craftsmen operating out of all the greatest kilns of the day took everything great that the Tang started and brought it to a new level. A new level of sophistication in design, materials, and firing.

09:00 As far as tea becoming central to formal and everyday Chinese etiquette, the Song dynasty is when it went to even greater heights. Although it may have started to become widespread during the Tang, by the Song, normal rules of hospitality dictated you served your guests tea. And on certain holidays and other auspicious days, perhaps an ancestor's birthday, you served tea and even offered it up to your dearly departed.

THE TEA HISTORY PODCAST BOOK 1
PART 7

09:27 | With tea now firmly inserted into the daily picture, it created an additional layer of lǐmào or etiquette to go with all of the other Chinese cultural niceties that had accumulated since Zhou Gong's time.

09:42 | Let's look at Cài Xiāng first. He was the Lù Yǔ of his day. And I guess you could call him the Wáng Xīzhī of his day also. You all remember Wáng Xīzhī, China History Podcast episode 96. So great was this man's calligraphy that the Taizong emperor, Li Shimin, requested a copy of Wáng Xīzhī's most famous work, the Lántíngjí Xù, be buried with him in his tomb.

10:09 | Cài Xiāng was, with Cài Jīng of Huīzōng's time, one of the greatest calligraphers of his age and some say the whole Song Dynasty. He lived from 1012 to 1067, dying a year after the Battle of Hastings to give you a little time stamp.

10:26 | The other three most famous Song calligraphers always mentioned in the same breath with Cài Xiāng were Sū Shì, Huáng Tíngjiān and Mǐ Fú. When talking about Song calligraphy, plenty of Chinese can rattle off the names "Sū, Huáng, Mǐ, Cài"

10:43 | Cài Xiāng came from present-day Pútián 莆田 in between Quánzhōu and Fúzhōu in one of the world's true tea paradises, Fujian Province. He served as an official during the time of the Rénzōng emperor. This was also the time of Ōuyáng Xiū who we featured in episode CHP-71.

THE TEA HISTORY PODCAST BOOK 1
PART 7

11:03   Cài Xiāng is most famous for his calligraphy and his work called the Chá Lù 茶录, The Record of Tea. This, along with the Cha Jing, the Classic of Tea, are among the most important of all the many tea treatises.

11:18   The Chá Lù is divided up into two parts. Like the Chá Jīng, which Cài Xiāng freshened up a little, it adds more narrative to the tools and ways to prepare tea. One thing he was adamant about was to stop impregnating the smell of the tea cakes with this camphor wood. He was a purist like Lù Yǔ when it came to adding stuff to the tea leaves. Both were both very strong advocates for drinking tea by itself, without the distractions of additives or scented packaging.

11:49   The whole fashion of using a bamboo whisk to whip the tea into a froth was an activity that was very popular during the salad days of the Song. I'd go so far as to say THAT was their signature contribution to Chinese tea culture.

12:06   The swells of the day in all the great cities famous for high concentrations of literati, used to hold these dòuchá contests. They were also called míngzhàn or tea wars. Míng being the name chosen for tea instead of cha. A zhàn is a battle. To dòuchá translates loosely to have a tea struggle or a tea fight.

12:32   On a simple level it was sort of like an Iron Chef kind of a contest to see who could prepare the best tea. One would face off against their various opponents and you'd put that mǒchá powder in that cup. Then with whisk in one hand and pot of boiled water or a ewer in the other, you'd start mixing it up, getting it just right and then you presented your bowl of tea to the judge of the contest.

12:58 Tea aficionados and everyone in Fujian province might be cringing at my completely stripped-down description of Song *dòuchá* tea contests. Actually, the whole matter was slightly more complicated. In these dòuchá events it wasn't enough just to offer up a tasty drink. The raw material was usually a very high-end tea cake. The contenders would grind their respective tea cakes into a powder using the tea utensils of the day. The ground tea powder was placed at the bottom of the tea bowl. Then using a ewer, a vessel to pour water, with one hand they poured and with the other hand they whisked.

13:40 When done up right and whisked perfectly, the froth on the tea was white or greenish white. The judge would check the whisk and tea utensils for any traces of water left on them. And these amateurs and masters who contended all had their own stylized ways to enhance the whole tea-making experience. And I'm sure when you had all these witty minds in one room together, the poetry, repartee and wit was probably flying thick and fast.

14:13 And if you're going to whip that tea up into a nice froth of white or greenish white color, nothing is going to look better than a lustrous black color tea bowl to complement the tea. That white against black really popped. To facilitate this, one of the calling cards of the

THE TEA HISTORY PODCAST BOOK 1
PART 7

Song Dynasty was born. This was their black color Jiàn ware. It came from Jiànyáng in Fujian province.

14:42 Jiàn ware wasn't all black. Little touches of color would be added that inspired poems and made these tea bowls coveted and most sought-after by collectors during the Song and a thousand years later.

14:56 The most prized decorations were called names like Tùháo zhǎn or Hare's fur or Dàimào zhǎn or Tortoiseshell, Zhègū bān which was partridge feathers. Another popular design was Yóu dī or oil droplets. In the Song dynasty, tea ware went from being a utilitarian object to a something collectors were willing to pay a lot of money for.

15:23 By the way, the reason why the Tùháo zhǎn or Hare's fur design was considered the best was because Emperor Hūizōng himself said so in his treatise that we're going to talk about next episode. If the Jiàn ware was inscribed on the bottom with the words Gòng Yù, then that meant the piece was tribute ware and not your average run of the mill stuff. The emperor didn't just get the best tea. He also got the best tea ware.

15:50 And just because you couldn't afford the finest Jiàn ware didn't mean you were excluded from enjoying this favorite Song Dynasty pastime. This *dòuchá* custom was popular with the masses as well as the swells. When this Jiàn ware made, it across the East China Sea and into Japan it created a sensation.

THE TEA HISTORY PODCAST BOOK 1
PART 7

16:10 In fact so much so, that whenever I see any black colored tea ware, I instantly associate it more with Japan than I do China. But it all started in the kilns of Jiànyáng in tea heaven, Fujian Province.

16:29 Some would argue this, but the ceramics from the Song period are the finest and most prized of everything China has ever put out there. We discussed Yuè ware, Xíng ware, Dìng ware and Jiàn ware. There was also another icon of Song ceramics, Qīngbái porcelain.

16:46 Song Qīngbái porcelain. That was good stuff. It was almost translucent but much less fragile than it looked. The color was a white or greenish white as the name *qīngbái* suggests. Qing is green and bai is white. Qīngbái in the Song was the prelude to the Ming dynasty blue-on-white and the Qing Guǎngcǎi 广彩 that used multiple colors on a white ceramic canvas.

17:15 There were many tea stories from the Song about these *dòuchá* events. Cài Xiāng once faced off against the noted literatus and calligrapher Sū Shùnyuán. In this story, Cai Xiang chose the better tea but Sū Shùnyuán brewed his tea with the more superior Zhuli water, Cai Xiang using an inferior but still top-drawer Huiquan Spring water. As the story goes, Cai Xiang lost the contest. Water, the mother of tea, could make or break your tea experience.

17:49 There was a newcomer in town during the Song dynasty. This was when Fujian Province started wearing its crown as the producer of the greatest teas. Tea culture in Fujian got itself noticed during the Song.

 THE TEA HISTORY PODCAST BOOK 1
PART 7

They originated the whole dòuchá custom that caught on in all the other provinces. Even Emperor Huīzōng. He loved to participate in these contests. This little bit of cha wenhua, tea culture, all started in Fujian. In the time of the Northern Song, people began to notice the tea masters in Fujian did something special with their tea leaves.

18:29　Tea bushes in Fujian aren't any different than the tea bushes in Sichuan. The terroir was different of course but in Fujian, they did things different. The tea growing masters in Fujian are going to create a whole new category of tea called Wūlóng that is going to take the country by storm and become the preferred kind of tea of artists, literary types and elites all over.

18:55　Tea had gotten big enough in Song China where the government began to take an even more active role in the trade. The Cha Ma Gudao we discussed in previous episodes, the Ancient Tea Horse Road. We saw how this trade route did so much to bring tea, Buddhism and some elements of Chinese culture to the Tibetans and others beyond China's far west borders. But it was carried out on a very small scale and though the job got done, it was very high cost, dangerous and logistically inefficient. The geopolitical dynamic of the times called for a little more aggressive action by the government with regard to the tea-horse trade.

19:39　Do you remember from previous episodes CHP-28 on the Northern Song Dynasty and that four part series on Emperor Huīzōng? One of the major headaches of the Song emperors from Zhào Kuāngyìn, the founder, all the way to Hūizōng was that they all had to deal with a lot of aggressive and murderous barbarians surrounding them on three sides. We remember that the Song government used old ways to humor the hordes surrounding them. They bought them off, married their daughters off to chieftains and khans, paid massive tribute, played one tribe off against the other and used all kinds of ways going back to the Han emperors to try and keep everyone at bay. They were able to do this to some extent through trade and diplomacy.

20:27 But in order to show they meant business, the Song military had to constantly be on alert and ready to carry out a show of force whenever these Tanguts, Jürchens, Uighur's, Khitan and Mongols too started getting designs on China. All of them were constantly probing China's sedentary soft spots, looking for some sort of advantage.

20:51 The Song government badly needed these people of the steppes because of the demand for horses. During the Song the need was greater than ever before in China's history. Foot soldiers were at a terrible disadvantage against mounted warriors.

21:07 The government early on, in the reign of the Zhēnzōng emperor 997-1022, began to lay the groundwork for government intervention in the tea-for-horses trade. And even though this brick tea was made with the least desirable tea leaves and contained stems and was terribly bitter compared to the good stuff, the demand

THE TEA HISTORY PODCAST BOOK 1
PART 7

for this tea, bitter or not, from the Tibetans and other border peoples was no less than the Song military's insatiable demand for their horses.

21:37 That was a fair trade, I think. Tea for horses. Both sides had something the other wanted. Over time they had established market prices for everything. About 130 lbs. of brick tea, 59 kilos, got you one horse. This clean and honest business was quite a contrast with eight centuries later when the British traders were engaged in the tea business.

22:03 Most of the tea in Sichuan and Yunnan ended up being processed into this brick tea and shipped from Yǎ'ān, near Chengdu, westward to Lhasa. But no matter how much tea they could pick, process, package and transport to the Tibetans and others to the west, it wasn't enough. The Song needed hundreds of thousands of horses. Five million pounds of tea, if they had that much production, at 130 lbs. per equine specimen yielded only 38,461.54 horses. The people up in Mongolia, Manchuria, Qinghai, they didn't have this problem. That's why they couldn't be beat. The Song military was able to subdue the Tanguts of the Western Xia for a while. But amongst the Northern Song emperors there was no Hàn Wǔdì or Táng Tàizōng, no great warrior emperor to conquer these troublesome people to the north and to the west.

23:07 But this trade in tea for horses at least kept the Song Dynasty in the game. They could never get enough horses out of the Tibetans. And their enemies certainly

THE TEA HISTORY PODCAST BOOK 1
PART 7

weren't going to trade horses. You don't see the US military selling F-22 Raptors to their enemies. Horses were the advanced weaponry of their day so why should the Jürchens sell them to their rival to the south? But what the Song government was able to procure certainly aided in the preservation of the dynasty. I'm telling you, the Song horse purchasing department really cleaned the Tibetans out.

23:40 Initially set up in 1007 under Zhēnzōng and institutionalized under Shénzōng in 1074, the Tea & Horse Agency based in Sichuan was the Song office tasked to fight this losing battle. The reforms surrounding this office and how it was staffed and operated was one of the reforms championed by Wáng Ānshí. Remember him? We mentioned Wáng Ānshí before. He was the great reformer during the Song. Six government-run horse markets were created and operated efficiently in the southwest of Sichuan to deal with their Tibetan counterparts.

24:19 So tea, innocently enough, because people who came in touch with it loved it so much, continued to play a role in not only China's daily social life, but because of export demand, it brought income into the royal coffers that allowed the brilliant lights of the Song Dynasty to keep burning bright.

24:40 I think this is as good a spot as any to wind things down and call it a night. We'll keep this going next time with more Song Dynasty antics. Didn't get to the Yuan this time, not that there was a whole hell of a lot to say. But

 THE TEA HISTORY PODCAST BOOK 1
PART 7

next time we'll get to that as well as all the profound changes that will happen in the world of tea during the early Ming Dynasty.

25:01 OK, that's all I got for you this time. Laszlo Montgomery here signing off from the town they call the city of Los Angels. Come back next time, ya hear, for another full-flavored episode of the Tea History Podcast.

The Tea History Podcast
Book 1 Part 8

SUMMARY

Buddhism continues to embrace tea even further during the Song Dynasty giving rise to the term 茶禪一味 "Tea and Chan Buddhism are one taste." More Huizong, white tea, Japan's Myōan Eisai, and then we'll close with an introduction to Wulong (Oolong) Tea and the emergence of the Wuyi Mountains in Fujian province as a tea powerhouse.

TRANSCRIPT

00:00 Hey everyone, I'm back. Laszlo Montgomery here with Part 8 this time of The Tea History Podcast.

00:08 In the Song Dynasty, tea had established itself as a component of the *Kāimén qījiàn shì*, the Seven Necessities of Daily Living in China. The original six were firewood, rice, oil, salt, soy sauce and vinegar. Back in times before the Song, if you woke up on a deserted island, you had to have those six things in your household. But now in the Song, the seventh thing you couldn't do without became tea. That's how important tea had become in China.

00:42 Teahouses were now commonplace in China. It started in the Tang, maybe the Sui. But the number of teahouses in China during the Song exploded. And once the teahouses proliferated as much as they did, they in turn

THE TEA HISTORY PODCAST BOOK 1
PART 8

served like a bellows to stoke the fires for the emergence of new kinds of Chinese tea culture.

01:05 Every city in China had their own little take on tea. Song dynasty tea culture drew from all these individual customs and practices from not only the palace in Kaifeng but also these individual tea cultures that developed in the great cities along the Yangzi and in the watery worlds of Zhejiang and Jiangsu. In these teahouses, the whole culture of *dòuchá* would be practiced throughout the Song dynasty.

01:35 Chán Buddhism in the Song reached a golden age, if you'll again let me use that worn-out overused cliché. The whole notion of Chán Buddhists embracing tea so fervently as an aid in meditation had already gained national prominence under Chán Buddhist Master Xiángmó of Língyán Monastery at Tàishān, the sacred Mount Tai near Jǐnán.

01:57 He was one of the best-known Chán Masters of his age. The Kāiyuán Era of the Tang. This was the most splendid period of the most splendid time in the Tang Dynasty. These were Emperor Xuánzōng's best years. It was supposedly Master Xiángmó Zàng who used his prestige as Chán Master at such a sacred spot at Mount Tai to propagate the benefits of drinking tea to stave off sleep during meditation and as an aid in getting through the evening when fasting.

02:32 Such words praising tea from someone as revered as Chán Master Xiángmó of Língyán Monastery was quite an endorsement. This was sort of like an official sanction, but it's just a legend, like so much of the history of tea. And whether or not this whole story is true remains to be historically verified.

02:53 The old saying Chá Chán Yīwèi (茶禪一味) "Tea and Chan Buddhism one taste" was already a well known saying by the Sòng dynasty.

03:02 The Buddhist monasteries held tea so close to their bosom and were enthusiastic proponents of all things great about tea. They lived amongst a population that, I guess you could say, was rather Buddhist at the time. It can't be denied that monasteries were a walking talking PR department for the merits of drinking and savoring tea.

03:26 Some might say Chinese tea culture really spiked during the time of Huīzōng. Again, go check out that China History Podcast four parter on his life, CHP episodes 132 to 135. Many high profile luminaries of the Song who I mentioned, Cài Xiāng, Cai Jīng, Sū Shì and others, throughout their career extolled the virtues of tea and wrote poems and calligraphy inspired by the taste and aromas of tea.

03:58 But when it came to culture, no one during the Northern Song dynasty was bigger than Huīzōng. Tea culture in the Northern Song hit a high note during the first half of Huīzōng's reign from 1100 to 1126.

 THE TEA HISTORY PODCAST BOOK 1
PART 8

04:13 | He took everything Lu Yu said and like Cài Xiāng, added his two cents worth. Like Lu Yu he gave, in twenty steps, a state of the art commentary on tea's history, how to grow it, the conditions you need, how to make it, assess it, grind it and so on and so forth. Huīzōng's masterpiece was called the Dàguān Chálùn. The Treatise on Tea, also called the General Remarks on Tea. Hūizōng published this during the pleasant part of his tragic reign in 1107.

04:49 | One of the things about Hūizōng that would have been unheard-of prior to his time was that he occasionally used to enjoy preparing tea for all his councilors. When they'd get together on official business or after hours, this is the kind of thing Hūizōng liked to do. As in all the arts of the time, this emperor loved to be looked upon as the final arbiter in what was art and what was good taste.

05:16 | White tea makes its debut on the tea stage around this time. Hūizōng had a section of his Dàguān Chálùn where he says,

05:25 | *"White tea is different from all others and deemed the finest. With wide-spreading branches and thin shiny leaves, the trees grow wild on forested cliffs. Their product is very sparse, however, and there is nothing one can do about it. Four or five families on the Baiyuan tea estate have some trees of this kind, but only a handful of them come to leaf, so no more than two or three bagful's can be gathered each year. Both shoots and leaves are small; steaming and firing them is rather difficult; for if the temperature is not*

110

THE TEA HISTORY PODCAST BOOK 1
PART 8

> *exactly right, they will taste like ordinary tea. Thus, a higher order of skill is needed and the drying must be carefully done. If everything is exactly as it should be, the product of such trees will excel all others."*

06:19 | You see, it was during the Song that masters figured out the youngest buds would produce a unique taste as far as mildness, subtlety and refreshing taste. Huīzōng wasn't pulling your leg. It was indeed hard to get and because the raw material was limited, so was the supply. It's called white tea because so young are the buds used that are picked that they still have these tiny white hairs on them.

06:47 | I've read this white tea of the Song was not the same as the white tea we're familiar with in our day. That was a creation of Qing Dynasty masters in the late 1700's and into the 1800's.

07:02 | In the last ten years or so, white tea has been marketed in the US in all kinds of forms by the tea and beverage industry. It's hailed for its ability to help you with weight loss, lower your blood pressure, give you healthier bones and skin and of course, because of all the antioxidants, it also has the same cancer preventative properties as green tea. White tea, because it has the absolute minimum amount of processing involved in taking the tea leaves to the final product, retains the highest level of antioxidants.

THE TEA HISTORY PODCAST BOOK 1
PART 8

07:36 Because of the chemical EGCG, mentioned in Tea History Part 2, epigallocatechin-3-gallate, researchers in Germany have produced studies showing white tea helped people lose weight. Five white teas that you may have heard of are Silver Needle, Long Life Eyebrow, Tribute Eyebrow, White Peony and Snowbud. I randomly checked an online tea store and saw Yin Zhen Silver Needle tea going for $30 per quarter pound, so $120 per lb. All the way from Zhenghe County to your door. Zhenghe and Fuding are the two places most famous for that Northern Fujian white tea.

08:18 With regard to the best tea bowls, Hūizōng was always chasing the thinnest, most delicate bowls. In his Dàguān Chálùn, he says,

08:28 *"The best kinds of tea bowls are very dark blue – almost black. They should be relatively deep so that the surface of the liquid will attain a milky color, and also wide to allow for whipping with a bamboo whisk."*

08:43 And as for the whisk, Hūizōng explains,

08:47 *"This should be made of flexible bamboo; the handle should be heavy, the brush like slivers light, their tips sharp as swords. Then, when the whisk is used, there are not likely to be too many troubles."*

09:01 Emperor Hūizōng, everybody. He didn't get to drink too much tribute tea in his last years.

THE TEA HISTORY PODCAST BOOK 1
PART 8

09:07 | Teas scented from flowers were another Song innovation. For the first time, teas scented with jasmine, rose and Osmanthus started showing up. Osmanthus is known as guìhuāchá in Mandarin. Today one of the great health drinks in the American tea industry.

09:26 | The government didn't only muscle in on the tea and horse trade. Tea had become important and sophisticated enough whereby the government, in all its wisdom, decided a system needed to be created to standardize the grading and quality of teas produced in the market.

09:43 | Not surprisingly, the most sought-after teas in the Song Dynasty were the ones whose leaves came from trees or bushes growing in the shadows of China's most sacred and illustrious mountains.

09:57 | The Lu Yu of Japan lived during this time of the Song. Again I don't want to get too deep into the history of tea in Japan. But it's important to know of Myōan Eisai. I mentioned him in Part 2. He lived 1141-1215. Eisai had multiple claims to fame. He is most credited with bringing green tea to Japan from China. He also studied the Rinzai school of Chan or Zen Buddhism that had been around since the Tang dynasty. It wasn't one of the larger sects in China but it sure caught on big in Japan.

10:32 | Eisai, he made his first trip to China in 1168, a Buddhist pilgrimage of course. He stayed in China for twenty-three years and returned to Japan not only with Chan Buddhist scriptures but tea seeds and the latest tea

THE TEA HISTORY PODCAST BOOK 1
PART 8

cultivation know-how. He planted these seeds in the Uji Hills just outside Kyoto.

10:53 For the rest of his days, Eisai propagated a lot of what he picked up in China after two decades of tea drinking. The whole idea about the Japanese tea ceremony as art and all the unique rituals and aspects of Japanese tea culture are said to have begun with Eisai's return from China in 1191. The Heian Era had just ended and this was the Kamakura period one year before Minamoto no Yoritomo, a name no less great in Japanese history as Tang Tàizōng is to China.

11:29 Let me read a poem by the Japanese Buddhist monk Myoe. It's called "The Ten Virtues of Tea" and shines a light on what tea, by the Song, meant in Japan society. Myoe's ten are:

11:43
> *Tea has the blessing of all deities*
> *Tea promotes filial piety*
> *Tea drives away evil spirits*
> *Tea banishes drowsiness*
> *Tea keeps the five internal organs in harmony*
> *Tea wards off disease*
> *Tea strengthens friendship*
> *Tea disciplines body and mind*
> *Tea destroys the passions*
> *Tea grants a peaceful death.*

12:15 I'm sure it sounded better in Japanese.

12:17 Let's finish off with Wūlóng tea. Between now and the

THE TEA HISTORY PODCAST BOOK 1
PART 8

end of this series, I'll try and give you a nice general overview of all the main teas. If you like tea and just want to learn a little more to expand your awareness, I hope this show offers you something useful. The list is very long of tea experts who write blogs, books, run teashops, online stores. Some have YouTube Channels and Facebook and Twitter accounts. You can really learn a lot fast and get right on it. Let's look at Wūlóng.

12:49 I heard three banal versions of how this tea got its name. *Wū* means black. *Lóng* means dragon. This tea is so good it's in a class by itself. Of the five categories of tea, white, green, yellow, red and pu-erh. A sixth one had to be added just for Wūlóng. It wasn't green and it wasn't red or pu-erh.

13:10 Nowadays black tea and Pu-erh tea are used interchangeably. But Oolong, it was somewhere in between. And that spectrum of how oxidized the tea masters allowed the leaf to get varied anywhere from 10% to 85%. So the tea masters in all the great Wūlóng growing tea gardens in Fujian, Guangdong and Taiwan, have all kinds of ways to work their leaves to give their tea its unique everything.

13:43 In the beginning there was Běiyuàn tea from Fujian. This was brick tea from the Tang that became one of the earliest Yùchá or imperial tribute teas for the emperor. Hūizōng himself mentioned Běiyuàn tea as superior in his Treatise, the Dàguān Chálùn. This Běiyuàn tea was made into tea cakes called Lóngfèng Tuánchá: Dragon-Phoenix Tea cake. These weren't bricks. They were cakes

THE TEA HISTORY PODCAST BOOK 1
PART 8

that might fit in the palm of your hand, again, with a nice ornamental wrapper. This is one of the calling cards of Song Dynasty tea culture.

14:23 When tea bricks sort of became passé, the good people there in Běiyuàn needed to come up with an encore to their once famous product: Lóngfèng Tuánchá. They came up with this new kind of partially oxidized tea that, although processed in a laborious fashion requiring a few extra steps, yielded a particular flavor as yet never tasted.

14:50 Back in the old days when Westerners were just starting to learn about tea processing, the word fermentation got bandied about as the chemical process that turns the leaves from green to black. But fermentation, as you remember from high school microbiology 113, only takes place where there's no oxygen.

15:11 Oxidation, as the name suggests, requires oxygen. When you break open that Lipton tea bag and see that tea, that is a fully oxidized black leaf. If you don't oxidize it or as they used to say in the trade, don't allow for fermentation, then you will have green or white tea. Black tea is fully oxidized.

15:35 Wūlóng tea. That's somewhere in between. And just how in between is the difference you can taste from tea garden to tea garden.

15:46 I don't like to generalize but in general, if you want to compress all the different kinds of Wūlóng tea into three

116

main kinds, first you have the renowned Wǔyí Rock Teas of the Wǔyí Mountains, Wǔyí Shān, in northern Fujian.

16:03   Then there is Tiěguānyīn or Iron Buddha or Goddess of Mercy tea. I'm sure you've had it before. Guānyīn, in Buddhism, helped the needy. If you were down and out and needed a miracle, you prayed to Guānyīn, the goddess of mercy as she is sometimes referred to. Tiěguānyīn tea comes from Ānxī in the south of Fujian. This is just north of Xiamen and west of Quánzhōu.

16:31   The third kind of Wūlóng used to be known a century ago as Formosa Wūlóng. This is the Wūlóng tea from Taiwan. In a class by itself.

16:42   One of the tell-tale signs of Wūlóng tea are the edges of the leaf. When you look closely, after the leaves have been steeped, the edges have a slight russet color to them. This is part of that magic worked into the leaves by the master artisans who make Wūlóng.

17:04   For Wūlóng tea, the yield plucked will be greatest in the spring but it's the leaves picked in the autumn that are considered the most fragrant. Don't forget the six steps to drinking Tiěguānyīn: observe, listen, view, smell, taste, appreciate.

17:25   As I said in a previous episode, the Wǔyí Mountains are located in northern Fujian, not far from the border with Jiangxi. This area is a UNESCO World Heritage site. The tea makers in Wǔyí Shan aren't going to wow the tea drinking world until the end of the Ming, beginning of

THE TEA HISTORY PODCAST BOOK 1
PART 8

the Qing. But their green tea, though still processed in cake form in the Song, by imperial decree one day, will be morphed into this special loose-leaf tea that the Wǔyí Shān area will become esteemed for.

18:01 | This very special tea is called Yán Chá or Rock Tea. Rock tea because the original trees grew out of these rock cliffs that made up the historic tea producing area of Wǔyí Shan. The Fujianese tea craftsmen of the late Song and early Ming, it seemed, weren't completely familiar with the pan firing technology that had been mastered by the producers across the border in Anhui.

18:29 | They had learned that when you pick the leaves and allow them to whither a bit in the sun, get them nice and pliable and loose, if you fire them or shāqīng in Mandarin, kill the green, you can halt any further chance of enzymatic oxidation of the leaves. That's why they're green. But if you don't fire the leaves or steam them, they start turning black on you.

18:56 | These chánóng, or tea farmers, up in the Wǔyí Shān area of Northern Fujian, either on purpose or by accident, figured out how to control the level of oxidation through the application of heat at critical times. They learned how to wholly or partially oxidize the leaves as they wished, to coax that very particular flavor out of these *Camellia sinensis* leaves.

19:26 | The most famous Yán Chá or Wǔyí Shān Rock Teas have names like Dà Hóng Páo, Tiě Luóhàn, Bái Jī Guān, Shuǐ

THE TEA HISTORY PODCAST BOOK 1
PART 8

	Jīnguī as well as Shuǐ Xiān, Bā Xiān and Ròu Guì.
19:41	In this little corner of Fujian everything that happened, geologically over millions of years, allowed the soil, the climate, the altitude to offer optimum conditions to grow tea.
19:56	And today's Wǔyí Shān tea growing area is broken down into three main categories. These are Zhèng Yán Tea, Bàn Yán Tea and Zhōu Tea. Zhèng Yán grows in the rocks in the highest peaks of the picturesque mountains. The Bàn Yán Tea grows in the foothills surrounding these rock mountains. The Zhōu Tea grows near the banks of the two rivers that wind through the Wǔyí Shan area, the Zhōu and Bā Xiān Rivers.
20:29	It takes seven stages of processing for your average Wūlóng tea. Withering, tossing and bruising, oxidation, fixing, rolling and forming, drying and firing. So easy to name those steps. It's not the steps but how they perform each step. That's where individual craftsmanship takes over. Like craft beers. There is no limit to how you can subtly manipulate the process to derive a unique tea tasting experience.
21:04	Besides the soil and climate, how much you let those leaves oxidize and how you worked the leaves during the process is what determines the outcome. This whole way that leaves from a *Camellia sinensis* bush or tree turn into the high quality teas we know today is not an intuitive process at all. That's why it took so long for those outside China to figure it out.

 THE TEA HISTORY PODCAST BOOK 1
PART 8

21:33 | As we can see from these past episodes, it took the Chinese centuries to get everything just right. We've seen how tea evolved from the crudest, most bitter brew, so bitter tea's Chinese name shared the Chinese character for a bitter vegetable.

21:50 | Between the time of the ancient Bā and Shǔ States in Sichuan through the Qin, Han, Tang and now the Song, tea evolved in fits and starts into this, now very refined and sophisticated level in the Song.

22:07 | Not only were these Wūlóng tea masters of Fujian blessed with land that had the perfect terroir, they were also most expert and innovative in working with the leaves. Famous tribute tea villages dotted Wǔyí Shan in the north and in Ānxī in the south where Tiěguānyīn is made.

22:29 | Tea didn't come to Taiwan till the early 18th century. But when it did and a few years after those tea trees planted their roots in that nice soil of Nántóu, Jiāyì and Huālián Counties, the masters there also turned out quite a magical Wūlóng tea that would gain world acclaim.

22:50 | We'll come back again and look at Wūlóng and many other kinds of teas. Wūlóng tea is special and it's during the Song that Fujian teas sort of muscle their way past the established players and really came to the fore. Nowadays, especially in the health products industry, Oolong tea is often touted as an aid to weight-loss and a remedy for a number of afflictions or maladies.

THE TEA HISTORY PODCAST BOOK 1
PART 8

23:16 In the Ming and afterwards, it seems all that mattered was Fujian province.

23:23 In the next episode the Ming Dynasty founder, Zhū Yuánzhāng, is going to make an imperial edict that says henceforth tea should be packed in a loose leaf form and not into these brick shapes anymore. You'd think, with everything we know today about tea that this idea should have come a lot sooner. Alas, the whole notion of loose tea like we know and love it today only began with the Ming Dynasty, the second to the last of Chinese imperial dynasty going back to the Qín. That's what we'll look at next time.

23:57 For now, this is Laszlo Montgomery signing off from LA in El Estado Dorado. I hope you'll find it in your heart to do the right thing and consider joining me next time for another delicious episode of the Tea History Podcast.

The Tea History Podcast
Book 1 Part 9

THE TRANSCRIPTS

SUMMARY

The epic story continues after all the great advances in tea production and tea culture in the Song. After surviving the Mongol Yuan Dynasty Camellia Sinensis experiences revolutionary improvements with the founding of the Ming Dynasty by Zhu Yuanzhang. Now tea starts to become more familiar to us after the Hongwu Emperor demands all future tribute teas must be sent in loose-leaf form. With loose leaf teas came greater demands for tea-ware. The history of the kilns of Jingdezhen is introduced, along with their calling card: Blue and White porcelain, China's first global brand. Other innovations such as teas scented with flowers and the Tea Manual of Zhu Quan are also introduced.

TRANSCRIPT

00:00	Hey Everyone, Laszlo Montgomery again. Tea History Podcast episode 9 this time. The focus today will be on tea during the Ming dynasty.
00:10	Blue and white porcelain. That's one of the icons of the Ming. Today we'll look at that too, as well as the town that made it famous.
00:20	We left off last time in the Song dynasty and saw how tea progressed since the time of the Tang. Mǒchá, tea powder, Cài Xiāng, Huīzōng, Eisai, Myoe and the new Song tea culture.

THE TEA HISTORY PODCAST BOOK 1
PART 9

00:33 And from the day Zhào Kuāngyìn founded the dynasty, China was surrounded by these tough guys who were always trying to use their brawn and fighting abilities, not to mention surplus horses, to overwhelm the Song. The Khitan Liao first humbled the Song. Then the Jürchen Jīn knocked out the Khitan and as an encore they went and finished up the Northern Song. And then finally the end came for the Jīn in 1234, 1-2-3-4, The Mongol forces ran roughshod over the Jürchens and thirty-seven years later in 1271, Kublai Khan founded the Yuán dynasty.

01:14 And the Yuan dynasty was not a golden age for tea in China. It was a golden age for laying low and waiting for this tempest to pass. Ninety-seven years the Mongols ruled China. They didn't drink tea the way the Chinese did. They stuck with their strong brick tea and they liked it mixed with cream or mare's milk and with a little salt thrown in. The way they did it in the Song with the ground tea powder, the whisk and the frothy whipped texture was right out as far as the Mongols were concerned. I'm sure this isn't true in every case, but *dòuchá* tea contests weren't a popular pastime with the Mongol nobles and soldiers.

01:58 But one change was just starting to happen in the world of Chinese tea during the Southern Song and into the Yuan. This was the introduction of brewing tea from dried loose tea leaves. A new method of processing tea called *chǎoqīng* had been invented. To *chǎoqīng* the leaves involved a new kind of drying which used a pan or wok to fry the withered leaves of the freshly picked tea. The previous system of roasting and steaming, though it

THE TEA HISTORY PODCAST BOOK 1
PART 9

	worked, was a little harsh on the leaves and it was easy to burn or scorch them.
02:36	For green tea, you needed to heat those leaves right away or else they'd start oxidizing like an apple. But this *chǎoqīng* method halted the enzymatic oxidation in its tracks. Although it was an improvement on past and heating methods, this chǎoqīng process still needed a couple of centuries before it was perfected.
03:00	This oxidation was good for tea but bad for things like fruit, shrimp, potatoes, bananas and avocados.
03:08	While China's tea culture languished under Mongol rule, the Japanese had no such problem. Despite the two massive Mongol invasions, rebuffed by the Kamikaze winds of 1274 and 1281, the Mongols were unable to do to Japan what they did to China. So while China was under the Mongol yoke, the Japanese thrived and prospered in their national tea culture. The 13th and 14th centuries were not the best of times in China for tea. But for Japan, this was the period when the distinctly Japanese tea ceremony was further developed and almost perfected.
03:47	As I said, the Yuan didn't last even a century. And even when Kublai Khan reigned, he was no Hūizōng when it came to imperial patronage of tea culture. And without a patron like the emperor, it's hard to keep a thriving national tea culture going. So although it was perhaps a dark age, it's not like it was pitch black. No one in China was giving up on tea just yet.

THE TEA HISTORY PODCAST BOOK 1
PART 9

04:11 One good thing though. Thanks to Mongol and other intrepid traders as well as the whole Pax Mongolica, among the commodities being traded from west to east was cobalt. In this way, China got a first look at this substance that became THE essential ingredient for the blue pigment that would become so famous in the Ming Dynasty.

04:36 The cobalt came from Iraq and Iran, though during the early Ming cobalt was discovered in China. Zheng He also brought this Persian and Iraqi cobalt back to China in greater amounts during his travels to Hormuz during a few of his seven voyages. The Chinese material didn't yield as rich of a blue as the material transported from the Near East. So think of the Yuan dynasty as a transitional period in the history of tea.

05:07 When Marco Polo wrote about his time in China during the period of his service in the employ of Kublai Khan, he hardly mentioned tea, if he mentioned it at all. And if you listen to the venerable China scholar Frances Wood, Kublai Khan never even mentioned Marco Polo.

05:24 Anyway, the Yuan was the dividing line between the supremacy of compressed tea and the triumph of loose tea leaves.

05:34 And this brings us to the Ming Dynasty, 1368-1644. The Ming was not a dark age for tea. Loose leaf tea is going to become the standard. The whole oxidation process is going to be figured out towards the end of the dynasty and then perfected during the Qing, allowing black tea

THE TEA HISTORY PODCAST BOOK 1
PART 9

to be unleashed on the world.

05:56 | The later discovery of black tea is going to do wonders for China's border trade. They had the system down pat as far as making these bricks and tea cakes but there was still spoilage and mold problems because of the harsh climate. The tea bricks and cakes, still produced from processed green tea, also didn't hold up well in foul weather.

06:20 | But now, with the emergence of black tea and the whole oxidation process understood, this is going to open up a whole new world as far as getting tea shipped over long distances, with less spoilage which meant higher profits.

06:35 | And we know after hearing it a hundred times at least in these podcasts, the Ming dynasty was founded by Zhū Yuánzhāng who reigned from 1368 to 1397. Along with Liu Bang who founded the Han dynasty, Zhu Yuanzhang was one of two dynasty founders who rose from humble non-aristocratic beginnings. He's also known as Ming Tàizǔ as well as the Hóngwǔ emperor.

07:03 | Lots of good things happened under his Hóngwǔ era. As I mentioned, loose tea became the norm. This happened in 1391, the 16th day of the 9th lunar month of the 24th year of the Hóngwǔ era. That's when the Ming founding emperor said, if you want to send me tribute tea, make sure it doesn't come in brick or tea cake form.

THE TEA HISTORY PODCAST BOOK 1
PART 9

07:28 In addition to this, new systems for grading tea were established and pretty much the foundations were laid for China's whole domestic and export tea industry for the next few centuries.

07:41 The whole idea of infusing loose tea leaves in all their glory meant that new kinds of teapots became necessary and began to emerge onto the scene. The early ones were relatively small since tea was always prepared in small amounts and drunk from small cups.

07:58 The Chinese figured out at once it wasn't good to leave the hot water in a pot of tea and steep those leaves too long. While everyone is enjoying their tea, too large a teapot meant that extra water would be sitting there just sucking up all the astringent tannins released from the steeping tea leaves. Anyone who left that Lipton tea bag in there too long knows what I'm talking about. With these new style teapots, all one had to do now was keep adding hot water to the loose tea leaves inside.

08:30 The purple zǐshā clay tea ware began in the Song but really became all the rage in the Ming. We'll talk about that. As far as tea-ware went, nothing was bigger than the story of Jǐngdézhēn. In fact, why don't we start right here with the history of this historic place. I have to guess that if any of you don't have any Jǐngdézhēn porcelain in your home, you at least drank out of their teacups or ate off their plates before at a Chinese restaurant or have seen them at someone's house.

THE TEA HISTORY PODCAST BOOK 1
PART 9

09:04 There are two stories about how we got the English name "China". One of them I've told in a previous China History Podcast episode, that the word China came from that Qin Dynasty name. Qín - China.

09:18 But there's another story and it concerns the ancient town of Jǐngdézhēn. Their history dates back to the Han, though the inhabitants of that area had been working with clay since 6500 BCE. The city was first called Xīnpíng then later became known as Chāngnán, Chāngnán Zhēn. Zhēn means town.

09:45 In China you either live in a *Shì*, a *Zhēn* or a *Cūn*. A city, a town or a village. So Jǐngdézhēn is Jǐngdé Town. Chāngnán Zhēn is Chāngnán Town.

09:59 The story goes that the earliest importers of Chinese porcelain got the word china from Chāngnán. So established was this part of northernmost Jiangxi province as a maker of porcelain, their ceramics became known as china ware with a small "c" of course. Just a story. Chāngnán - China. Hey who knows?

10:22 Chāngnán didn't become Jǐngdézhēn till the reign of the Northern Song emperor Zhēnzōng. He was the nephew of the founder and was the third emperor of the Song.

10:33 One of the five era names of Zhēnzōng's reign was the Jǐngdé Era, lasting from 1004-1007. Chāngnán was already an established go-to place for any and all porcelain ware. So it was there that the Song Zhēnzōng

THE TEA HISTORY PODCAST BOOK 1
PART 9

emperor called for imperial officials to be stationed. And their job was to personally oversee all the porcelain production earmarked for palace use.

11:03 And believe it or not, it stayed that way for 900 years. In the Song and Yuan, imperial agents would sort through the very best that all the different individual kilns had to offer. They'd be presented with the cream of the cream, and these imperial agents would select which pieces went to the capital.

11:25 In the early Ming, Zhūshān, or Pearl Hill, today a district of Jǐngdézhēn, a special ceramics operation was set up that produced porcelain ware exclusively for the capital. This place remained in operation up through the end of the Qing.

11:43 So although Jǐngdézhēn's history as China's Porcelain Capital goes back as far as the Tang or even the Han, it's in the Ming dynasty, again, 1368 to 1644, where Jǐngdézhēn porcelain first achieves notoriety and global acclaim.

12:02 And may I further add that in a way, Jǐngdézhēn porcelain was China's first global brand.

12:10 The treasures that came out of Jǐngdézhēn were prized in their own time by emperors and other royals. Even today, collectors fork over ridiculous sums of money for Jǐngdézhēn porcelain.Some of you may recall earlier in 2014 some Shanghainese pharmaceutical magnate named Liú Yìqiān paid $36 million US to purchase a tiny porcelain cup, 3.1 inches in diameter. This "chicken cup"

THE TEA HISTORY PODCAST BOOK 1
PART 9

as it was called because of the painted hen and rooster images was produced about a hundred years into the Ming Dynasty for the Chénghuà Emperor who reigned 1464-1487.

12:56 Jǐngdézhēn isn't just famous for being the exclusive purveyor of porcelain ware to the imperial family. Towards the latter half of the Ming dynasty, that's when the Europeans came calling for the first time. And the second they lay their eyes on this stuff, it's going to be a case of love at first sight. And Jǐngdézhēn is going to become the primary exporter to the world of one of China's signature product specialties. Japanese buyers bought from Jǐngdézhēn and even brought their own designs there to be produced for their market.

13:32 Even after the Hóngwǔ emperor died in 1398, there were still three hundred and five years to go before Böttger figures out the secrets of the seventy-two steps to turn kaolin mixed with ground china stone into a crystallized hard porcelain object. So Jǐngdézhēn is going to have one hell of a run between the Ming and the year 1703 in the Qing dynasty.

13:58 The reason the center of the porcelain world ended up in Jǐngdézhēn was because of the rich deposits of kaolin enriched clay that, because of the low iron content, was particularly white. In Mandarin this clay is called Gāolǐng. There's a Gāolǐng mountain there. Guess what mineral deposit it's loaded with? Then not far away were the Sānbǎo Mountains which were chock full of feldspar-enriched china stone, the other main component in making porcelain.

14:30 Today kaolin's largest application is in the paper industry where it's used as a clay coating for paperboard. But kaolin, this stuff was the best for making porcelain. Because of the inherent nature of this substance, kaolin, you could make a cup or dish or whatever, eggshell thin, translucent, just gorgeous. It was a pleasure to hold and to behold.

14:59 Porcelain produced out of Jǐngdézhēn was expensive but the mass-market export quality chinaware they also produced was affordable at the same time. This is going to be a key point because once tea gets enthusiastically embraced by the unwashed masses of Europe and America, everyone had to have one of these china tea pots. And not only that, once Zhu Yuanzhang, the Hóngwǔ emperor put his foot down and declared that henceforth tea should come packed loose and no longer compressed, these tea pots, gàiwǎns, and tea cups became perfect vessels to enjoy this new loose tea culture.

15:40 Though first begun in the Yuan dynasty, huāchá or scented tea, began to gain in popularity in the Ming as new ways to make these flower-scented teas are figured out. Fujian province, as usual, taking the lead. Loose tea opened up the door to all kinds of new processed teas like scented tea and tea blends that mixed different spices, fruits or other additives. I read that another use of scented teas was sometimes to disguise the aroma of otherwise inferior teas. If the leaves weren't quite up to

THE TEA HISTORY PODCAST BOOK 1
PART 9

	par or past their sell-by date, you could disguise the tea's shortcomings with a hint of jasmine, rose or osmanthus.
16:28	This was an old trick some Cantonese chefs picked up when they invented sweet and sour pork. The pungent viscous red-orange sauce would drown out any slight odors coming from three-day-old pork. The kwai-loh's had no idea.
16:44	Other places produced ceramics but only Jĭngdézhēn's designs became internationally renowned. Back in the Ming Dynasty, as far as China was concerned, the known world consisted of Asia, India, Egypt, Europe and East Africa.
17:02	If Jĭngdézhēn is China's most famous city for porcelain, Jĭngdézhēn's most famous porcelain, especially wherever tea ware was concerned, was their blue and white. Production began around 1340 at the tail-end of the Yuan dynasty during their last emperor, Huìzōng. Different Huìzōng from the stylish Northern Song emperor we featured in four parts and discussed last episode in Part 8.
17:30	So this porcelain ware in no time at all, in the years just before the Great Age of Discovery, became China's most well-known export. It was a huge hit in every market it appeared. Zheng He on his seven voyages spread a lot of this stuff around all over the place. People are still digging shards of these blue and white tea pots and tea ware out of the ground all the way into our day at all the places he visited, including the former Swahili Coast in

THE TEA HISTORY PODCAST BOOK 1
PART 9

east Africa. A lot of Straits Chinese families have some of these antique blue and white pieces that came from the Zheng He era.

18:10 The custom was continued during the Ming that dictated when the emperor died, his porcelain ware was never used again. I don't know if it was buried with him in his tomb or what they did with it. But whenever there was a new emperor on the throne, the kilns of Jǐngdézhēn would suddenly get very busy.

18:30 For all Imperial ware, the custom was always to print on the bottom of the cup, dish, bowl, vase or whatever, the era name of the emperor. So, for example, during the reign of the Yǒng Lè emperor, all the porcelain would be inscribed with Dà Míng Yǒnglè Zhì, made in the Míng Yǒnglè Era. When you look at antiques you can check the bottom to see if it has these inscriptions.

18:58 Most of the time, it'll probably just say Zhōngguó Zhìzào: Made in China.

19:05 Nowadays the workshops in Jǐngdézhēn are mostly all modernized, fully automatic, computerized and state of the art. Tens of thousands of people clocked in every day at the kilns of Jǐngdézhēn during the Ming. The growth of the operation there grew spectacularly during the Ming period and even more during the Qing. And though the workshops produced all manners of categories of porcelain products, it was tea that was the driving force behind a great deal of this growth.

THE TEA HISTORY PODCAST BOOK 1
PART 9

19:36 | Every age has their definitive tea manuals. The Tang had Lù Yǔ's Classic of Tea, the Chá Jīng. In the Song, you had Huīzōng's Tea Treatise and the Chá Lù of Cài Xiāng. In the Ming, there was Zhū Quán's Chá Pǔ of 1440 and Gù Yuánqìng's Chá Pǔ of 1541. Same Chinese name but different English names. One of those things.

20:02 | Zhū Quán had the good fortune to be the 17th son of the Ming dynasty founding emperor. He got to live a very fun and productive life. He was a master of the arts, music and Daoism. He was also a military man but had been muscled out of any possible political role by his older brother Zhū Dì, the later Yǒnglè emperor.

20:51 | So Zhū Quán, knowing a losing battle when he saw one, stayed clear of politics and lived the life of a gentleman scholar. And with all this time on his hands, he freshened up all the work of his predecessors and brought tea culture one step closer to perfection with his work describing the latest in tea preparation, utensils and further tips on water.

20:51 | But most of all, this Tea Manual written by Zhū Quán was the first of the tea classics that was written during the time of loose tea leaves. He was in lockstep with his father, the Hóngwǔ Emperor, on this matter. Brewing loose tea was a radical departure from the established ways of doing things.

21:10 | Zhū Quán also offered up commentary on past tea classics. After the Hóngwǔ emperor's decree saying no more tea bricks, it was left up to the son Zhū Quán to explain the

THE TEA HISTORY PODCAST BOOK 1
PART 9

new culture to an eager audience. Zhū Quán had written in the Chá Pǔ that the way of preparing tea from tea cakes profoundly impacted the taste of the tea. The only way to get the true inherent taste of the tea leaves was by brewing the processed loose tea in boiled water.

21:43 And like Lu Yu, Zhū Quán was a strong advocate for ambience. Where you were drinking the tea and the conditions in which you were drinking was also important and contributed to the overall experience. All these great tea masters had reasons for their favorite kind of tea ware. Zhū Quán believed white tea bowls was the way to go if you wanted to truly appreciate the tea. So we can rest assured that had Zhū Quán been alive in the Tang he would have favored Xíng ware over Yuè ware. The cast iron tea pots that today no self-respecting tea master would be without, those too were given a big boost by Zhū Quán. Boiling your water in those kinds of pots on your charcoal stove was the way to go back then and still today. These too are available at your local tea shops and in most of the online stores. They ain't cheap but I saw a nice collection of 27 oz. cast iron tea pots online going for around fifty bucks. I've also seen these things go for hundreds of dollars.

22:48 The other Chá Pǔ was written by Gù Yuánqìng. He lived 1487 to 1565, the time of the Zhengde and Jiajing emperors. I'm just going to mention a couple of these tea classics. By this time in the Ming dynasty, books were being printed in every direction with every would-be tea expert weighing in about the best ways to prepare, serve and drink tea.

THE TEA HISTORY PODCAST BOOK 1
PART 9

23:14 | Gù Yuánqìng's Tea Manual, like Zhū Quán's focused solely on loose tea. I guess maybe in this new age of tea new advice needed to be dispensed. Gù Yuánqìng's book mainly talks about the Eight Requisites for Tasting Tea. All seems so common sense but I guess not back in the mid 16th century. A few of the main points from this work: Use good quality tea and fresh spring water to make it. Pay attention to how you boil the water and infuse the tea leaves. Don't skimp on the utensils. Use the best there is.

23:50 | Then as far as tasting the tea. You don't hē chá or drink tea. You pǐn chá. To *hē* is to drink. To *pǐn* is to sip. Now I didn't know this when I began my tea studies in Hangzhou in 2013. This character *pin*, three mouth characters, *sange kou*, in a pyramid, one on top of the two. I always knew it meant "thing" like in *chánpǐn* or *pǐnzhǒng* but it also has another meaning: to sip. So Gù Yuánqìng in his Tea Manual made an extra effort to emphasize that you pǐn your chá.

24:32 | What other words of wisdom from Gù Yuánqìng? Watch the water temperature. If you boil it too long, it releases oxygen and causes the water to taste flat. And choose your tea companions carefully. Nothing enhances the pure enjoyment of the tea experience than good and interesting friends to share it with you. Gu's eighth requisite is to put your heart into the preparation of the tea and don't forget the tea snacks.

25:02 | There are so many of these tea books. Some we remember, some we don't. So much was changing. I know we don't

THE TEA HISTORY PODCAST BOOK 1
PART 9

look at the 14th and 15th centuries as recent times but for China's long history going back forty-two hundred years to the legendary Xià in 2194 BCE, the Ming was modern history. Zhu Yuanzhang only founded the Ming dynasty six and a half centuries ago. So you can see in the context of forty-two hundred years, the changes happening in Ming dynasty tea culture sort of fall under the category of recent Chinese history.

25:40 I guess the main thing you can say about tea and the Ming dynasty besides the emergence of loose tea and Jǐngdézhēn onto the world stage, would be that the tea ceremony, the tools of the trade, the utensils used, the processing ways and the general way we casually and formally drink tea all sort of become recognizable to us in the Ming. The evolution wasn't complete, but if today's tea masters had to do a gongfu tea ceremony to someone back in the Ming dynasty, they'd probably do ok. I guess once you got rid of the bricks and the need to grind the tea, the ceremony became a much more aesthetically pleasing experience.

26:24 Well, I don't want to say anything but we're in stoppage time so we may as well draw the curtains and call it a night. Laszlo Montgomery signing off from Los Angeles, Cali beseeching you once again to come back next time for another gratifying episode of the Tea History Podcast.

The Tea History Podcast
Book 1 Part 10

THE TRANSCRIPTS

SUMMARY

More Ming Dynasty tea history this time. Further innovations from China's tea artisans further improves the taste and experience of tea. The famous "zisha" clay teapots and teaware from Yixing are introduced as well as their role in the Gongfu Tea Ceremony. As the second half of the Ming Dynasty starts to wind down, the Europeans will soon be knocking on China's door. They too will discover the goodness and greatness of tea with historic consequences.

TRANSCRIPT

00:00 | Hey Everyone, Laszlo Montgomery again. Tea History Podcast episode 10 this time. More Ming dynasty stuff for you.

00:08 | Last time we got a nice intro to the great porcelain capitol of China, the city of Jǐngdézhēn…just a little south of the Yangzi River and west of Lake Poyang in historic Jiangxi province. Without any further chit chatting or yammering, let's keep going with the Ming Dynasty.

00:29 | Tea leaves had gone from being boiled during the time of the Tang to being crushed and ground to powder in the Song and finally in the Ming, steeping leaves in boiled water. Zhǔchá to mǒchá to pàochá.

THE TEA HISTORY PODCAST BOOK 1
PART 10

00:44 Beginning in the 14th century, the Ming rulers took a long time to finally fight off those Mongols and subdue them. This wasn't done until the time of Yŏnglè. Horses were no less important than ever before and something as important as the tea-horse trading system remained critical to the dynasty's well-being. In the Ming the Horse Trading Offices in Shānxī and Shănxī managed the trade.

01:11 The Ming government controlled all export of tea. Same thing when Mao took over in 1949. The market prices determined by the Ming government were 120 jīn of tea for a superior horse, 70 jīn for an average one and 50 jīn of tea for an inferior horse. These were the prices set by them. And to enforce this, they really cracked down on anyone trying to export tea outside the system.

01:41 A jīn is 1.1 pounds or 0.6 kilos. Jin is sometimes called a Chinese pound. It's also referred to as one catty.

01:52 The tea tax, in place since 973, the final years of the Song founding emperor Tàizǔ, by the end of the Ming and into the Qing was gradually reduced. By this time it was acknowledged that tea had become such an important daily use item, taxing it was causing undue hardship on the peasants and commoners.

02:13 Once loose leaf tea became the accepted norm, and I don't know who would want to keep using bricks or tea cake, it led to an explosion of new tea varieties. Many of the famous teas we drink today came out of the Ming dynasty.

THE TEA HISTORY PODCAST BOOK 1
PART 10

02:29 Do you remember from a previous episode a "famous tea" is what these former tribute teas are called today. We'll go over them later on in the series. Brick tea was still manufactured in the Ming. The Chinese may have turned their back on it, but the Russians and other Central Asian people continued to demand this form.

02:49 The whole custom of xǐ chá started in the Ming during the loose leaf era. This involved washing the tea. Xǐ means to wash. This involved pouring boiled water over the leaves first. Then you dumped out this water and the leaves were now considered cleaned. Or cleaner than they were before. You always want to do this when using loose leaf tea.

03:15 I couldn't find the source again after I read this somewhere, but there was an old saying: "Always offer the first pouring of tea to your enemy." In other words, when you make that first pour that tea isn't cleaned and there might be who knows what in there. The belief was if you poured hot water and then dumped it, whatever was in there in terms of dust, impurities, microbes or whatever undesirable things, you dealt with it. So that's why you got that saying, don't dump the tea, serve it to someone you don't like.

03:49 Let's talk about Yíxìng teapots for a bit. We discussed Yíxìng in an earlier episode. That's the area near Mount Gùzhǔ where the famous Purple Bamboo Tea or Zǐsǔn Chá came from. Lù Yǔ wrote a good portion of the Chá Jīng, The Classic of Tea, over here.

THE TEA HISTORY PODCAST BOOK 1
PART 10

04:11 Yíxìng's former name was Yángxiàn. You remember Yángxiàn tea that inspired Lú Tóng to write the poem "Seven Cups of Tea."

04:21 This place is going to become even more famous because of these teapots that came out of there. What Jǐngdézhēn was to porcelain ware, Yíxìng was to those small purple clay teapots. There was a third center in China for tea ware. This was in Déhuá in central Fujian, west of Quánzhōu. Like Jǐngdézhēn, they had no shortage of kaolin material around Déhuá and they too developed quite a porcelain legacy.

04:49 In and around Yíxìng they have this clay called zǐshā. Zǐ means purple and shā means sand or anything granular. I think I mentioned the area around Yíxìng had been making these purple clay pots as far back as the Song. But it's in the Ming where these things come into their own and become wildly popular.

05:12 The clay comes in three basic colors depending on how much oxidized iron is concentrated in the mixture. They can either be a coffee or cream color, red or purple-brown. The clay coming out of Yíxìng, all lead-free, comes in five colors: red, black, purple, green and yellow-green. But you could combine these different colors and add all kinds of pigments to it to get a nice wide range of earthen hues.

05:41 It's a very laborious process to get the raw material from the ground into a moldable clay. What you have in the end, and perhaps the best selling point about zǐshā ware

THE TEA HISTORY PODCAST BOOK 1
PART 10

is that because there's no glaze, the clay is porous and thus, over time, it absorbs the oils and flavors of the tea that are poured inside. This is why you don't really want to mix teas in a single zǐshā teapot. The zǐshā teapot you use for your best Pu-erh, you don't want to use it with your freshest Tiěguānyīn.

06:16 That's one of the special things about zǐshā. All that flavor absorbed over the years actually seasons the teapot and this in turn enhances the taste of the tea later on. In fact there's an old saying or story that if you used one single zǐshā pot to brew one single type of tea for long enough, after a while you didn't need to add tea leaves. The pot itself would give off the flavor or essence of the tea.

06:46 So with these things never, never wash them in soap. You have to raise these teapots. Like a Neopet. Remember them? In Chinese this is called Yǎng hú, to raise the teapot. You gotta take care of it to allow it to realize its greatest potential one day.

07:07 Collectors love Yíxìng tea ware. Since you're only supposed to limit the use of one Yíxìng teapot to one selection of tea, it is common for true tea experts to have multiple teapots for multiple teas. Collectors will have both decorative and practical Yíxìng teapots. The decorative ones of course for display only and the simpler more practical ones for actual use. All the tea people I've met over the years all swear by Yíxìng purple clay tea ware as the best vessels for serving tea. They're all individually hand crafted, not thrown on a

THE TEA HISTORY PODCAST BOOK 1
PART 10

potters wheel. Back in the day the craftsman who made the teapot would sign it or inscribe his chop on the bottom.

07:57 Yíxìng teapots are like jade, pearls and other collectibles. There are good ones and bad ones. Unless you know what you're doing, it's easy to walk into a teashop and get ripped off when you go buy one. There's a lot of stuff to know but the main things you want to ensure is that the tea pours smoothly and no dribbling from the spout. The inside and outside of the teapot should be smooth. The lid should be nice and tight. In a random check of a hundred web sites I bookmarked, I saw Zisha teapots going for as low as $53 to as high as $250 with the average price for a 4.5 oz. to 7 oz. teapot going for about $150 or so.

08:45 If you've never seen Yíxìng teapots before, at first you might not find them particularly attractive. Most of them have no decorations and are simply an unglazed solid earthy color. But the experts swear by them. They are small, functional, and perfect for when you're enjoying some real nice stuff. It's said there are about 125 individual steps to making a top-end handmade Yíxìng purple clay teapot.

09:17 And for the gōngfu tea ceremony that we'll talk about later, this is the only way to go. Because they don't dress themselves up with fancy designs or colors, the thing about these small purple, reddish, brownish teapots is the form, shape and perfection of the body.

THE TEA HISTORY PODCAST BOOK 1
PART 10

09:36 And again, the mass popularity of Yíxìng tea pots came about as a direct result of the Hóngwǔ emperor's edict calling for loose tea leaves to become the standard in the land. These and other 5 to 7oz. teapots became perfect vessels for these kinds of leaves. And with the introduction of this unique Yíxìng ware, collectors on a budget and those who have millions to spend developed a passion for this tea ware. This passion will remain wildly popular and carry into the Qing and into our present day.

10:13 The gōngfu tea ceremony went hand in hand with the introduction and popularization of Yíxìng tea ware. Yíxìng tea ware isn't really meant for green tea. There's no law that says you can't do it, but I can't remember ever seeing green tea being used in Yíxìng ware in a gōngfu tea ceremony. They're meant for either Oolong or pu-erh tea.

10:36 The gōngfu tea ceremony is like the opposite of dunking a cheap tea bag into a thick 10 oz. C-Handle ceramic mug filled with boiling water. The name gōngfu means this is a kind of activity requiring time, skill and effort. Not easy or simple to do. It was ritualized, stylized and ceremonial yet at the same time not so stuffy and hoity toity that the masses couldn't join in and participate as well. And because it was called gōngfu cha, as I said it meant it took a little extra effort to make it. So there's an implied respect and humility in the whole ceremony between the one serving and the others being served.

THE TEA HISTORY PODCAST BOOK 1
PART 10

11:30 | The Chinese gōngfu tea ceremony isn't nearly as stylized, ritualistic or symbolic as the Japanese Cha no Yu. Nothing like it at all. It's simply a way of preparing the best possible tea you can afford or get your hands on in the most precise manner to derive the best possible outcome. So many variables are at work at the same instant. Knowing how to manage everything is what separated the experts from the novices. How much tea to scoop out? How hot should the water be? How long do you brew? What water to select?

11:57 | In the typical gōngfu tea ceremony there are about a dozen things you'll need to do it up right. I've been to tea shops everywhere and you can always get these tools of the trade in a set. Or you can buy them separately. Many of the online purveyors of fine and distinctive whole leaf teas also sell tea ware and utensils and other fine accouterment.

12:19 | Yíxìng ware is the way to go so you will need a tea pot and tea pitcher to decant the tea into. An iron pot with a charcoal stove would be nice but in a pinch there's are always hot plates or worst-case electric kettles to boil the water. Get something with a thermostat so you can monitor the water temperature. Different tea leaves require different water temperatures.

12:44 | You need three small cups. These tiny cups, you've seen them before, they're called pǐnmíngbēi. So fanciful. Pǐn, remember, to sip. Míng, from History of Tea Part 1, míng is one of the ancient characters for tea and bēi is cup. A sipping tea cup. Three cups works best. Three is the perfect number in that it represents heaven, earth and oneself. So in the gōngfu tea ceremony it's always best to have one person doing all the gōngfu and two guests. No rule says it has to be this way so don't stress it.

13:21 Besides cups, you will also need various utensils to do your job. A strainer to place over the tea pitcher to avoid any leaves being passed from the teapot. There's a tea towel to keep all the spills and drips under control. You have a *cháhé*, a little scoop that measures out the tea leaves from your storage. This scoop is used to transfer the tea leaves into the Yíxìng teapot. These elongated scoops can be as simple or ornate as your heart desires. One of the customs after the server has scooped up some tea leaves calls for everyone to first check out the cháhé scoop and admire the leaves in their dried form.

14:05 You'll also need a pair of tongs to handle the pǐnmíngbēi teacups. You don't want to be handling these tiny cups with your fingers. There's also a tea pick. Just something to poke into the tea spout in case anything gets stuck in there. You never know.

14:21 Many of these utensils are the same or variations of the utensils Lù Yǔ said you had to have in your tea toolbox.

14:29 And the stage to perform all the steps is called a *chápán*, a tea tray. This is a nice flat surface, with drainage that allows all the liquids to fall below the tray surface into a compartment that collects the water. All the action happens on top of this tea tray. The sky's the limit on what these things can cost. I've seen some pretty top rate ones in my day.

14:56 The gōngfu tea ceremony does not have to use Yíxìng tea ware. There's also the gàiwǎn method. Gài means lid and wǎn means bowl. These lidded cups were designed for loose leaf tea. It's a covered tea bowl and you put tea leaves in it and then you can either drink from the tea bowl or in the case of gōngfu chá, you use it as the vessel to steep the tea leaves instead of another vessel like an Yíxìng clay pot or something like that. The gài for the wǎn, the lid for the bowl, also has a secondary role as a strainer to hold the tea leaves in while you pour or drink. And as a lid, it also keeps the tea hot. These are wildly popular and, may I say, I'm more of a gàiwǎn person myself.

15:45 The gōngfu tea ceremony, developed in where else, of course, Fújiàn province. Always those guys. It became a very popular social custom in the Ming dynasty. If you want to go on YouTube or Youku you can see hundreds of these videos showing how it's done.

16:03 I've counted about twelve basic steps to this process. Each step in the gōngfu tea ceremony has a special name that draws from poetry, legend, history or something dramatic. This ceremony is mostly about enjoying the best teas possible using the most careful and deliberate preparation. And of course enjoying it with people you love or admire.

THE TEA HISTORY PODCAST BOOK 1
PART 10

16:30 | The gōngfu tea ceremony, like any tea drinking experience, can be enhanced greatly with some relaxing or inspirational ambience and a couple of good friends and some smart conversation. Remember from a previous episode, water is the mother of tea. Don't skimp. If you're going to pay fifty bucks for an ounce and a half of some top drawer oolong or pu-erh, don't use water from the tap. And for crying out loud, remember what Lù Yǔ said and don't get it from the village well. Go get yourself some good spring water in a bottle. Just remember to recycle the bottle when you're finished. Filtered water will also do, but not recommended if you can get the real thing. If you live in the mountains with a nearby unpolluted stream, hey baby, you hit the jackpot.

17:19 | Remember the old Chinese saying: Three times boiled water is dead water. Only boil enough water to do what you gotta do. Try not to re-boil the water.

17:30 | So tea took a nice great leap forward in the Ming Dynasty. Again we have the dynasty founder Zhū Yuánzhāng to thank for that. Everything is starting to look more recognizable to us. By the time of the Ming Wànlì Emperor who reigned 1573 to 1620 it had been forty-three hundred years since Shén Nóng first noticed the goodness of tea.

17:55 | It had evolved from a crude bitter medicinal brew to something barely palatable until the Sui and the Tang when suddenly the masters of tea figured out better ways to process the leaves and turn this bitter brew into a pleasing beverage. Once philosophers, artists and poets

 THE TEA HISTORY PODCAST BOOK 1
PART 10

of the Tang and the Song became hooked, they turned the appreciation of tea drinking into an entire lifestyle and pastime that many around the world enjoy today.

18:17 The lands bordering China and the lands bordering the lands that bordered China were also hooked on tea. They didn't go in for the fancy ceremonial stuff. For these people outside China proper, life was rough, and tea played a daily part in their very survival. I mentioned what a big difference Princess Wénchéng was to the Tibetan people when the legend says she brought them the nutritional benefits of tea to the Himalayas.

18:44 But there was a big world out there. As big as it was, there was more to it than Central Asia, the subcontinent and the east coast of Africa. In the time of the Wànlì emperor, it had already been a century since the Age of Navigation. And now Western people in greater numbers than when Marco Polo came, are going to start knocking on China's door and announcing themselves for the first time. And these, well, to the Chinese anyway, foul smelling, crude and barbarian men too are going to get themselves hooked on tea. And when they do, the world will never be the same again. Well, China's world that is. And this story is going to be shelved until next time.

19:29 We'll look at the arrival of the Europeans next episode and what that's going to mean for China and the whole tea world. Tea doesn't stop evolving in the Ming dynasty. We'll also look at advances in tea that happened during the Qing.

19:41 | We still have a whole lot more history and general info about tea. So if you've been looking at your watch these past ten episodes and wondering how much longer. I promise you the story is about to get much more interesting. We're always guaranteed a few yucks whenever East meets West. So please don't abandon ship just yet.

20:01 | Once again mes amis thanks so much for listening, streaming, downloading however you found me. This is Laszlo Montgomery signing off from the city of Los Angeles here in the state of Confusion, wishing you all the best and it's my greatest of hopes that you'll join me next time for another sapid episode of the Tea History Podcast.

www.ingramcontent.com/pod-product-compliance
Lightning Source LLC
LaVergne TN
LVHW010331070526
838199LV00065B/5716